REACHING THE LEFT FROM THE RIGHT

REACHING THE LEFT FROM THE RIGHT

TALKING ABOUT SOCIAL ISSUES WITH PEOPLE WHO DON'T THINK LIKE YOU

BARBARA CURTIS

BEACON HILL PRESS
OF KANSAS CITY

ISBN—13: 978-0-8341-2202-4
ISBN—10: 0-8341-2202-2

Printed in the
United States of America

Cover Design: Chad A. Cherry
Interior Design: Sharon Page

Library of Congress Cataloging-in-Publication Data

Curtis, Barbara, 1948-
Reaching the left from the right : talking about social issues with people who don't think like you / Barbara Curtis.
p. cm.
Includes bibliographical references.
ISBN-13: 978-0-8341-2202-4 (pbk.)
ISBN-10: 0-8341-2202-2 (pbk.)
1. Christian life. 2. Church and social problems. 3. Christianity and culture. I. Title.

BV4501.3.C87 2006
261.80973—dc22

2006013681

10 9 8 7 6 5 4 3 2 1

CONTENTS

How can I repay the Lord *for all*
his goodness to me? . . . O Lord,
truly I am your servant. . . .
You have freed me from my chains.

—Ps. 116:12, 16

INTRODUCTION

When it comes to walking a mile in someone else's shoes, I'm qualified indeed. In fact, I've walked thousands of miles in all different kinds—from Birkenstocks to strappy high heels to clunky workmen's boots. I've done a lot of walking barefoot too!

My slogan's changed from "Life's too short for ugly shoes" to "Life's too long for painful shoes." I've grown up. I've changed. In 1987 I finally heard Jesus knocking at the door of my heart, and I opened it wide. I think He had been knocking for a long, long time. But once I was no longer alone, I realized that a lot of the walking I had done was in the wrong direction.

Most amazing was that the moment I became a believer, everything about me was instantly changed. Especially evident, since I had always been heavily involved in politics, was my transformation from an America-hating radical to a grateful patriot. Our mail carrier must have been thrown for a loop when, until it ran out, my *Mother Jones* subscription was joined by the *National Review*.

This change didn't sit well with the fourth-generation, ultraleftist California clan of my husband, Tripp. As his brother assessed the new family dynamics, "We might have been able to handle you two becoming born-again Christians, but not born-again Republicans."

He wasn't kidding.

Since we were living in probably the most fiercely liberal, cynical enclave in America—Marin County, California, just over the Golden Gate Bridge from San Francisco—his reaction was typical. We just didn't fit in anymore. Ah, but before long I remembered the place where I had spent my young adulthood. If any place could offer an antidote to the unwholesome climate we now realized we were in, it would be Virginia. Almost immediately we started making plans to move.

But our move didn't happen right away. For 16 years, though our house was on the market more often than not, things never worked out, and we were left waiting and wondering why.

During that time, Tripp and I continued to expand our large family, and I began to write. I now think God had a purpose in keeping us in California through those years. Because of my background, I understood completely the leftist point of view—but I needed more motivation to boost my ability to communicate to both sides. The years I spent writing conservative columns in an exceedingly liberal newspaper challenged me to develop my skills to reach the broadest audience even when dealing with controversial issues.

My writing was further enriched through the two years I served as editor for Focus on the Family's *California Citizen*, the state insert in their monthly national magazine. For this I thank Matt Kaufmann, under whose tutelage I grew enormously. Each month I dug deeply into a specific issue of concern to California families—abortion, gay rights, cloning—researching, interviewing, then producing a reader-friendly piece to bring families up to speed on the issues.

Focus on the Family eliminated the state inserts in 2002, just two months before our long-prayed-for move to Virginia suddenly and "coincidentally" materialized. It was as though we had been on a battlefront and God tapped us on the shoulder and said, "You may stand down now."

We moved cross-country in August 2002 (3,000 miles in eight days with 10 kids—but that's another story) and settled cheerfully into a culture where Christianity is mainstream and the Pledge of Allegiance is still OK.

Less than a year later, I flew to California to teach at the Mount Hermon Writers' Conference, the place where I have been nurtured and now help nurture other writers. There I met two editors from Beacon Hill Press of Kansas City—Judi Perry and Bonnie Perry (related not only by publishing house but also by their marriage to brothers). We were eating breakfast together one morning, and somehow by the last sip of coffee this book had been conceived.

I now begin to write, with gratitude to Beacon Hill and my editors, who trusted my experience and insights and gave me this opportunity to bring a message of hope: that if we understand the issues and develop true compassion, we might learn to bridge the communication gap—at least a little. We might begin to find enough common ground to speak in a way that brings people closer together rather than farther apart.

INCREASE YOUR COMPASSION

My conversion was so radical that it would be otherwise unbelievable—except that we know just how surprising and powerful God can be. In the beginning it was not my great wisdom that people were looking for when they asked me to share my story—I was so new to the Bible that I couldn't tell the Old Testament from the New—it was the drama they wanted to hear. Since the hope was that others might identify with my experience and put their faith in Jesus Christ, the audience was usually stocked with at least a few who looked as though they needed a message of redemption and renewal.

One time was different. I'll never forget it—looking out over a sea of "perfect" Christian ladies at luncheon tables and seeing no one who looked even remotely as if she needed to hear my message at all. I know appearances can be deceiving, but trust me—

one formerly wayward soul knows another when they meet. And that day there was not one there.

Seeing no one who needed my message certainly put a different twist on things. My pursuit of "freedom" had caused a lot of chaos in the lives of others, particularly my first two daughters. As a new creation in Christ, I had had no trouble accepting God's forgiveness and specifically repenting to those I had hurt. "Therefore, there is now no condemnation for those who are in Christ Jesus" (Rom. 8:1). I knew this deep in my bones before I ever recognized it as a verse in the Bible.

And yet suddenly and for the first time, at this particular ladies' lunch I felt ashamed of who I had been. What would these solid, faithful women think of the rose tattoo on my hand—would they understand it was less a decoration than a cry for help? And worse, what would they think of the awful things I had done?

I stumbled through the episodes that brought me to so many dead ends—my antiwar activism, my radical feminism, and my move from Washington, D.C., to San Francisco in 1972. My downhill spiral continued through welfare, drug addiction, sexual promiscuity, and my life as a "fag hag," the affectionate term for a woman who hangs out with—and in my case, lived with—gay men.

I shared how my life began to change when I called out to God for help in 1980 but how it still took two years working through 12-step programs and five years exploring the New Age movement before I found a true relationship with Him through Jesus Christ.

I had no idea what the Christian ladies would make of this crazy tale, so far removed from their experiences. *Lord, why in the world am I here today?* I thought as I finally sank into my seat. I only wished I could have sunk through the floor instead.

And perhaps it was beyond the pale. Perhaps it was a turnoff. Perhaps most of the ladies missed the point. After all, as it turned out, *I* had.

Finally one beautiful, grandmotherly pillar of the church swept over and grabbed my hands in both of hers. With her soft, cream-colored outfit and her cloud of silver hair, she might have been an angel. And certainly her message hit me like a heavenly salutation.

"I had to come and thank you," she said. "I know we're supposed to love the sinner and hate the sin, and I've always said I did, but now I know I've never loved them at all. Listening to your story, I realized how much I hated people like you. But now it's gone. I understand. I see the pain."

How I wish that kind of understanding could bridge the communication gap between the polarized platforms on either side of the most volatile issues of our times: feminism, abortion, homosexuality, stem cell research, euthanasia. How I wish each side could see the pain and humanity of the other!

We've all seen those ugly pictures of abortion proponents screaming at pro-life activists. Those images hurt. But then we've also seen the terrible pictures of certain so-called Christian leaders carrying signs that say, "God hates fags." Those hurt more.

They hurt especially because they play into the hands of so many who already hate Christians. They hurt because they don't communicate the good news of Jesus Christ but the bad news that some who profess to follow Him haven't learned to follow Him at all.

As *World* publisher Joel Belz has written, "No matter what expression it takes, the inclination to put someone else down is always ultimately rooted in our determination to lift ourselves up and then perch ourselves on some lofty and prominent peak."[1] Or as in the word picture I use to show my children the ugliness of spiritual pride—cutting off someone else's head to make yourself appear taller.

By contrast, the only true Christian response toward any issue must be based on humility. Scripture reminds us that "He must become greater; I must become less" (John 3:30). Good advice but tough to follow unless we realize that salvation doesn't give us the privilege of feeling better than anyone, no matter where he or she stands in relation to God's kingdom.

The fact is, God doesn't hate fags at all. In fact, if Jesus were here, He would probably lavish more time and energy on them than on straight folks. We would probably be bewildered and even angry—at least until we remembered that when He walked among us He chose to spend time with prostitutes and tax collectors. After all, as Jesus explained to His critics, He came for the sick, not the well (Matt. 9:11-12).

WHAT DOES GOD'S WORD SAY?

Even before Jesus was here to demonstrate the correct response to sinners, the Old Testament contained this warning:

"Do not be overrighteous, neither be overwise—why destroy yourself?" (Eccles. 7:16).

And from the New Testament:

"For all have sinned and fall short of the glory of God" (Rom. 3:23).

We destroy our credibility as followers of Christ when we rely on slogans or when we see ourselves as morally superior to those with whom we disagree. No matter how pure our lives, even an inkling of pride sabotages our ability to communicate the truth. How can we ever forget that virtually the only people who felt the harshness of Jesus' tongue were the religious legalists and Temple traders?

We modern-day followers of Christ don't follow His example much, do we? Busy with Bible studies, home groups, and who-knows-what-else—I've been in churches where believers were kept busy every night of the week—we barely have time to get to know the family next door, let alone the lesbian couple who just moved to the suburbs to get their adopted children into a better school system.

But do we want to?

Would you have wanted to know *me*?

I was that crazy acid-dropping hippie chick at the antiwar rallies, yelling obscenities about the country you love. I was the one calling cops pigs. I was the radical feminist pushing for abortion on demand and feeling pretty lucky we had succeeded when I needed one myself. I was the party-girl single mother whose children you felt sorry for. I was that welfare mom at the Laundromat scrounging through my bags for enough change to wash our clothes. I was that coworker who came in haggard and hung over each morning, only to go into inexplicable hyperspeed after taking a pill. I was the drugged-out "fag hag" crawling down the hall to curl up in a bedroom after partying with the gay guys in the Castro district of San Francisco. Crawling because—and not everyone even knows this happens to heavy drinkers—my legs would no longer carry me.

I was the cynic who hated Christianity and everything I thought it stood for—though truth be told, I really knew nothing about it at all. I was that enraged voice railing to "keep religion out of politics," accusing conservatives and traditionalists of hypocrisy. I was the sexual revolutionary who didn't think it was anyone's business who slept with whom. I was the angry feminist with the bumper sticker demanding to keep "the government out of my womb." I was the angry protestor against "censorship." I was the elitist who adored edgy movies and art—the more blasphemous the better.

Would you have wanted to know me?

If you saw me in need—as Peter saw the crippled man who begged every day at the Temple gate called Beautiful— would you have seen beyond the outer circumstance? Would you have seen as Peter saw that the crippled man didn't need money, he needed to walk? Would you have seen that though I was chasing the things of the world, what I needed was a healing? Would you have helped me?

These questions worry me. They worry me because I know that many God-fearing people had walked by that crippled man at the gate called Beautiful, either ignoring him or giving him money, which wasn't what he really needed. And many walk by people like me each day and miss the opportunity to heal.

I was 38 years old before I finally heard the good news of Jesus Christ. There were probably Christians around me too wrapped up in their religion to notice how much I needed what they had to offer—too comfortable in church life, too assuming that I was too tough a nut to crack, too focused on our differences and not the fact that in God's eyes we all fall short.

In fact, I met one just a few years ago when I was asked to speak at another ladies' luncheon where, as I greeted the women working in the kitchen, I noticed a familiar face I couldn't quite place.

"Remember me?" she said, smiling. I had to confess I didn't remember where I knew her from.

"Kimberly," she said. "We worked for the phone company in Corte Madera in 1979."

"Kimberly, I didn't know you were a Christian!" I said. And then there was an embarrassing moment of silence, as we both realized that's probably the last thing a Christian would want to hear. I mean, what if when we stand before our Creator there is a cloud of witnesses who became believers *in spite* of our neglect? I can almost hear them intoning the chorus, "I didn't know you were a Christian!"

But then again, when I think what a mess I must have been—with my daily hungover/hyper cycle plus my immodest wardrobe—I have a lot of compassion for Kimberly and any other Christians who had the opportunity but never approached me.

I just didn't look very approachable. Had they spoken to me of Jesus and His power to heal the brokenness inside me—which they might have guessed at even if they couldn't see—I might have answered them with contempt and scorn.

But who knows? No one ever tried.

I actually got sober while working at the phone company with Kimberly. It was 1980. I had just moved to Marin County after eight years of wild living and serial drug dependencies in San Francisco. As muddled as my mind was, I knew there was a better life for me and my two daughters north of the Golden Gate

Bridge, and I was desperate to find it. Miraculously, I was able to convince the landlord of a sweet little two-bedroom house—with a yard and everything—to rent to a single mom.

By the grace of God—a God I had not yet met—we were lifted from a second-floor flat in the graffiti-ridden and mariachi-music-soaked Mission District of San Francisco to a safe and cozy neighborhood where I could clip roses from my own bushes and my daughters could play in their own backyard.

It's called a geographic—when a drug addict grabs onto moving as a solution to the problems he or she faces. And for me, no matter how rosy things were looking, it didn't take long for me to realize that *inside* nothing had changed. Although I had shaken serial drug dependencies, I had never shaken my dependency on booze. Every night I went to sleep in a blackout, often not even remembering where I had parked my car.

It was waking up from a blackout 17 days after our move that finally brought me to my knees.

"God! Help me!" I cried. "I'm an alcoholic—I need help!"

I had never cried out to God before, never applied the label "alcoholic" to myself. If I had known any Christians, I probably would have allowed myself to be led to the Lord—or at least to church. I was scared. I was broken. My defenses were down.

As it was, I did my mom thing first, dropping my daughters off at school. Then, not knowing which way to turn—and also because I was on warning for absenteeism—I went in to work and blurted out my problem to my boss.

I'm astonished now that this is what I did. I mean, it made me so accountable. With my cover completely blown, everyone would be watching me. In this turn of events—as in the miracle of a 1980 single mother being able to rent a comfortable home in a quiet neighborhood—I see God's hand—protecting, guiding, loving me—even before I knew Him, even when I was most unlovable.

GETTING REAL

No matter how good a person you are, how well you've lived your life up until this moment, there is no insurance policy against sin.

True humility demands that we remember that each of us is just one heartbeat, one wrong decision away from a life of sin and completely dependent on the mercy of God to keep us in His grace. Spiritual pride only divides us from others.

I spent the morning crying, searching through the Yellow Pages under "alcoholism" for some place to get some help. One person I talked to suggested Alcoholics Anonymous (AA) and gave me a list of meetings. Somehow I muddled through the rest of the day looking forward to taking the first step toward a better life instead of looking forward merely to going home to drink.

Rumors flew quickly around my office, so I imagine by lunchtime everyone knew what had happened, yet even though there was at least one Christian there—Kimberly—no one really came alongside me to offer me support. No one suggested church or told me about Jesus. Not that I would have expected it—I was pretty much a Lone Ranger—but looking back, I think it would have been a splendid opportunity.

In AA they say every alcoholic has to hit bottom, and every alcoholic has a different bottom. I was lucky—or blessed—that I hadn't lost my job, my daughters, or my place to live. Having never heard of recovery or rehab, I didn't know I had an alternative but to go to work each day and go to AA meetings at night. So I got sober on the job.

Since the first year of learning to live without alcohol is an emotional rollercoaster—my own theory is that you stop growing emotionally when you start drinking, which meant that though I was 32 years old, I was 16 emotionally—I had many an on-the-job breakdown the first year. I worked in customer service under a lot of pressure, and some days all it took was one mean customer for me to snap. Then I would dash out of the office for the ladies' room. I would lock myself in a stall and cry and cry and cry. I've wondered many times since how different things might have been had someone followed me in and shared with me the "peace that passes all understanding."

But though no one reached out in that way, as I grew more stable, my coworkers were happy for me—and even threw me a surprise party for my one-year-sober anniversary.

During that first difficult year I learned to pay my bills on time, confronted the reality of my lack of mothering skills, and worked hard to become a better person. What helped was something I found in AA that I had never found in the outside world: unconditional acceptance. AA was a level playing field where people from many races, social classes, and backgrounds worked together to beat a common enemy: substance abuse. In AA I learned to take an honest look at the harm I had done to others and to make amends. I also learned to face the demons that had driven me to *anaesthetize* myself. When I remembered my druggie days, it wasn't as though I always sought the same kind. On the contrary, I got hooked on uppers, downers, and combinations. Obviously, the particular altered state didn't matter. I just wanted to be anybody but me.

That's because being me was painful. You saw the anger. Underneath it all was hurt. Maybe that's the part that's hardest for lifetime Christians to understand: those individuals who revel in sin—you know, those who thumb their noses at convention and seem to make a life goal of freaking out conservative, traditional types—are not as comfortable with themselves as they would lead you to believe.

WHAT DOES GOD'S WORD SAY?

"The LORD does not look at the things man looks at. Man looks at the outward appearance, but the LORD looks at the heart" (1 Sam. 16:7).

"Judgment without mercy will be shown to anyone who has not been merciful. Mercy triumphs over judgment!" (James 2:13).

My own background—the demons from which I was fleeing, the spiritual disease from which God would eventually heal me—included divorce, abandonment by my parents, an abusive foster home, sexual predators, and grinding poverty. And while material poverty can be alleviated by faith, hope, and love—in my childhood those qualities were in even shorter supply than money.

Typically, individuals who have been hurt as children make decisions based on protecting themselves. I decided not to feel, to trust only myself, to take control of my life, to hurt others before they could hurt me. From the outside you would have thought my heart was very hard. But that's because it was covered with scar tissue—you know, that glossy, too-tight tough skin that grows over a wound.

My guess is that the deeper the wound and the less healing attention it received, the worse the scar would be. The worse the scar, the more intense would be the effort to hide it.

My hurts took place in the 1950s, but today—with the growing rate of divorce and fatherlessness—there are more people like me than ever, people flouting convention, scoffing at the rules, looking uncaring and sometimes downright mean. These are people with scar tissue guarding their hearts, looking for increasingly more outrageous ways of signaling that they don't care.

RESOURCES

If you've been a Christian all your life and are unfamiliar with the struggles of those not blessed with growing up with a spiritual foundation, here is a must-read: *No Compromise: The Life Story of Keith Green*. This is a biography by Keith's wife about his journey through immorality and corruption to his salvation in Christ and complete dedication to Christian worship and evangelism. Though his life was cut short at 28, his music alone is a moving testimony to the power of God to reach the most unreachable.

Also worth reading is *Out of the Depths,* the original autobiography by slave trader

John Newton, whose dramatic conversion at sea resulted in the best-loved hymn of all time, "Amazing Grace." As one reviewer at <www.amazon.com> said, "This book broke scabs off of my heart that I thought were petrified!"

And who couldn't use a little more of that?

Talk about outrageous ways of signaling—you find the best examples in San Francisco. Several years ago when I lived in California and was on assignment for a parenting magazine, I took a few of my kids to the preview of *Toy Story II*. I've never been able to figure out where they get the audience for a preview, but there were some doozies there that night. I was particularly struck by a couple who sat a row in front of me and to my right. They were Goths, dressed all in black with big stomper lace-up boots and short, very black hair. The guy's neck above his black leather jacket was a massive tattoo all the way to his hairline and ears. His ears had many piercings, filled with heavy silver-colored rings. A heavier ring pierced the center of his lower lip. And then there was something I had read about but not yet seen in person—a row of bumps marching neatly across his forehead, designed from steel balls implanted under his skin.

The woman with him, bare arms bedecked with tattoos, was remarkable in her own right, but he was clearly the rooster to her hen, with much more to display. They were unsettling, to say the least—perhaps downright scary to many.

But obviously they were not scary to their eight- or nine-year-old daughter, whose dress and demeanor were completely normal. It was clear that she loved her mom and dad immensely, and when they looked at her, their eyes took on a tenderness any parent would recognize and understand. And I understood that there was our common ground—our love and nurture of our children, for I wasn't about to judge them as less capable of loving their child than I, even though we might look as if we were from different planets. And after all, they had taken their daughter to see not *Terminator* but *Toy Story II*, a movie with a beautiful message. And what caught my attention was the love between parents and child—the eye contact, the touches, pats, and smiles.

I wondered how many people might have written the parents off as hopeless. Who knows? Maybe the same number who wrote *me* off as hopeless.

I remembered taking my daughters to the movies in San Francisco and how I must have looked to people in my outlandish clothes and once-upon-a-time radical tattoos.

And I remember that it was my desire to become a better parent that brought me to the kinds of places where I eventually heard about Jesus.

The point is this: God has plans for people that we cannot fathom. And no one is beyond His reach.

Before I knew Jesus, I was not an easy person to love. The way I dressed and spoke, my interests and my attitude, might have turned you off. You would not have understood why having an abortion didn't take much of a toll on me. How could you understand that someone who had never known the love of a Heavenly Father, who felt like a throwaway herself, would have no concept of the sanctity of life? You might exhort and admonish me 'til the cows came home, but I could never have heard you. It would have been as though we spoke two different languages.

And yet there is the universal language of love. And had you noticed in the morning when my hands were shaking and taken them in your own, had you followed me to the bathroom when I cried, had you somehow allowed yourself to become a conduit for God's love, I know I would have felt it. And it might have been as though a wilted, stunted flower had finally felt the sun.

BUILDING BRIDGES

Discussion Aids

- ★ Try to see each person the way God sees him or her.
- ★ Remember: *There but for the grace of God go I.*
- ★ No matter how hard another's heart, keep yours tender.
- ★ Be as accepting and approachable as you can be.

* Pray to love the unlovable.

Action Points

If you find yourself reacting negatively to those who think or speak or dress differently than you do—and particularly to those whose appearance is meant to make an antisocial statement, try these activities:

* Cut out pictures of the types that make you feel uncomfortable—Mohawk haircuts and body piercings included. Hang them over your computer or kitchen sink or on your bathroom mirror—a place where they'll confront you all the time. Each time you look at them, try to see them more through God's eyes. Pray for them and those like them. Learn to love them as Jesus would.
* When you see someone you think would be hard to love, stop and pray. If possible, speak to the person: *What have you heard about the movie we're waiting in line to see? Isn't the lettuce looking fresh today?*
* If you work with someone shaky and unlovable, ask if he or she needs some help with his or her work. *Can I get you something while I'm out for lunch? Do you need someone to talk to?*

STUDY YOUR CULTURE

Any good missionary scrutinizes the culture he or she wants to reach. In addition to knowing about the language and currency, the missionary needs a fix on the prevailing customs, mores, and attitudes. Often the native values are markedly at odds with the values of the missionary. Sometimes they're downright repugnant.

But a missionary would be pretty ineffective if he or she couldn't get past repugnance to understand what makes this chosen mission field tick.

Which of us isn't on a mission field? And which of us couldn't profit from a little less *tch-tching* at the sorry state of our culture and a little better grasp of the current trends in attitudes and ideas? What *is* my next-door neighbor thinking? What's driving my plumber to midlife crisis? What's wrong with my son's college professors? What's eating my coworker with the Darwin fish-bedecked minivan?

In his excellent book *In, But Not Of*, Hugh Hewitt makes the point that every Christian needs to develop and use whatever gifts God has given him or her in order to arrive at the maximum level of influence. Only in this way, Hewitt argues, can we continue to spread liberty and thus the gospel.

I strongly believe that in order to maximize our influence, we need to speak in language people understand about things they understand.

From my own experience as a pagan—as well as my years as a Christian—I can tell you that many Christians come across as so culturally different from non-Christians that it's almost like an alien nation. In our pursuit of righteousness and sanctification, we sometimes set up so many protective barriers that we no longer have anything at all to talk about with our next-door neighbors.

While some would argue that this is not a bad idea—that Christians shouldn't have much in common with their neighbors—I disagree. Missionaries in foreign lands familiarize themselves with the native customs and try to immerse themselves—to the extent they can without compromise—into the daily lives of those they serve.

Our spirituality must find application in daily life and shouldn't come across as something that makes us exclusive or strange. Just as missionaries trust God to protect them, we can trust God to protect us.

Even if you've forbidden your children to get involved in Pokemon or similar trends that sweep through the younger generation, it's helpful to have a passing knowledge of what they're about. It's helpful to explain it to your children as well. And it's helpful to explain in such a way that they don't come across to their friends as uptight and judgmental but just matter-of-fact about how such trendy fare just doesn't align with our beliefs.

And what of adult fare? When *The DaVinci Code* was first published, like many Christians, after reading several reviews, I put it on my "Books I'll Never Read" list. My mind was made up that Christians should avoid like the plague a book that denied the divinity of Jesus and portrayed His relationship with Mary Magdalene as sexual.

However, since its publication on March 18, 2003, The *DaVinci Code* has been translated into 40 languages and has sold 17 million copies. A major movie is in the works, directed by Ron Howard and starring Tom Hanks—both well-loved movie icons. Clearly, the story has become a cultural touchstone, whether people actually believe its false premise or not.

As for me, I've finally ordered a copy and am plowing my way through it. Why? Because I realize that not having read it puts me at a distinct disadvantage should I ever have an opportunity to talk to someone who has. Because if I knew what I was talking about, I would have a starting point to launch a discussion about the spiritual truth versus the spiritual counterfeit. I would be ready to defend the divinity of Christ.

WHAT DOES GOD'S WORD SAY?

"Though I am free and belong to no man, I make myself a slave to everyone, to win as many as possible. To the Jews I became like a Jew, to win the Jews. To those under the law I became like one under the law (though I myself am not under the law), so as to win those under the law. To those not having the law I became like one not having the law (though I am not free from God's law but am under Christ's law), so as to win those not having the law. To the weak I became weak, to win the weak. I have become all things to all men so that by all possible means I might save some. I do all this for the sake of the gospel, that I may share in its blessings" (1 Cor. 9:19-23).

Familiarizing ourselves with the things of the world does not necessarily corrupt us if we are looking at them from a Christian perspective. It's simply doing our homework as missionaries of light in a dark world, using the current culture to spark conversations.

Compare our situation with that of Paul in Acts 17:16: "While Paul was waiting for them in Athens, he was greatly distressed to see that the city was full of idols."

It's frustrating today to see newspapers, magazines, movie marquees, and bestseller lists chock-full of questionable "religious" ideas and current objects of pagan worship: sex, drugs, materialism.

"So he reasoned in the synagogue with the Jews and the God-fearing Greeks, as well as in the marketplace day by day with those who happened to be there" (v. 17).

We do our best to share with those who will listen, those with whom we share some common language.

> A group of Epicurean and Stoic philosophers began to dispute with him. Some of them asked, "What is this babbler trying to say?" Others remarked, "He seems to be advocating foreign gods." They said this because Paul was preaching the good news about Jesus and the resurrection. Then they took him and brought him to a meeting of the Areopagus, where they said to him, "May we know what this new teaching is that you are presenting? You are bringing some strange ideas to our ears, and we want to know what they mean." (All the Athenians and the foreigners who lived there spent their time doing nothing but talking about and listening to the latest ideas.) (*Acts 17:18-21*).

Sounds like what our children must put up with when in high school and college.

> Paul then stood up in the meeting of the Areopagus and said: "Men of Athens! I see that in

every way you are very religious. For as I walked around and looked carefully at your objects of worship, I even found an altar with this inscription: TO AN UNKNOWN GOD. Now what you worship as something unknown I am going to proclaim to you" (*Acts 17:22-23*).

Paul familiarized himself with their territory and used this knowledge to seize their attention before diving into what he really wanted to tell them about: the Truth. Imagine if he had said, "Don't you know these idols are all false?" We have the same stultifying impact when we say, "Oh, the *DaVinci Code*? I didn't read it because it's full of lies," or "I didn't let my kids read *Harry Potter* because wizards are demonic." How much greater credibility would we have with nonbelievers if we could use the things that interest and influence them as springboards into spiritual conversations?

> The God who made the world and everything in it is the Lord of heaven and earth and does not live in temples built by hands. And he is not served by human hands, as if he needed anything, because he himself gives all men life and breath and everything else. From one man he made every nation of men, that they should inhabit the whole earth; and he determined the times set for them and the exact places where they should live. God did this so that men would seek him and perhaps reach out for him and find him, though he is not far from each one of us.

> "For in him we live and move and have our being." As some of your own poets have said, "We are his offspring" (*Acts 17:24-28*).

Now Paul contrasts the true God with the idols worshiped in the Athenian culture. Likewise, we can speak today of the distinctives that set God apart from the confusion of other objects of worship.

> Therefore since we are God's offspring, we should not think that the divine being is like gold or silver or stone—an image made by man's design and skill. In the past God overlooked such ignorance, but now he commands all people everywhere to repent. For he has set a day when he will judge the world with justice by the man he has appointed. He has given proof of this to all men by raising him from the dead (*Acts 17:29-31*).

Paul lets them know that now that Christ has died and risen, people no longer have any excuse to remain ignorant. Once they've been shown the truth, they must make a decision. Sounds a lot like the Four Spiritual Laws, which for many decades Campus Crusade for Christ has been using to bring people to Christ, and an important part of the Good News we bring people today.

> When they heard about the resurrection of the dead, some of them sneered, but others said, "We want to hear you again on this subject." At that, Paul left the Council. A few men became followers of Paul and believed (*Acts 17:32-34*).

Some sneered. When we share the gospel, we take the risk of people's contempt. But some became followers as well. And it's clear that to maximize our chances of being heard and understood, we need to start from the familiar base of what people already know.

As a Christian, you have a certain relationship with the media. Hopefully, your faith is not compartmentalized from your entertainment choices. Hopefully, you bring a certain Christian perspective to what you find there.

But for those without a spiritual foundation, the media represent the closest thing they have to a religion. Since we were made to worship God, those who don't know Him are all engaged in trying to fill the void one way or another—which explains the cults that grow around rock groups, tattoos, piercings, television and movie series, and books like *Harry Potter*.

Earlier I posed some representative questions: What *is* my next-door neighbor thinking? What's driving my plumber to midlife crisis? What's wrong with my son's college professors? What's eating my coworker with the Darwin fish-bedecked minivan?

The best place to find the answer to these and similar questions might be your local movie theater, where you'll find the wide-open masses eagerly absorbing Hollywood's eye-view of history, society, morality—and yes, spirituality.

Witness how one movie—*Saving Private Ryan*—awakened an almost-oblivious generation to the sacrifice of its fathers in World War II. Or the surge in belief in reincarnation following a slew of 90s films sentimentalizing loved ones returned from the dead.

Filmmakers like to claim—especially when they're under the gun—that movies don't influence but simply reflect the culture. They do both. And their power to change people's lives both individually and en masse is enormous.

Paul Harvey wrote,

> Nobody could have persuaded a generation of Americans to produce a baby boom, but Shirley Temple movies made every couple want to have one. Military enlistments for our Air Force were lagging until almost overnight a movie called *Top Gun* had recruits standing in line.

Wholesome themes and wholesome dividends are not things we associate with Hollywood these days. While family fare like *The Sound of Music* and *Ben Hur* once swept the Academy Awards, since the late 1960s, with *Midnight Cowboy* and *The Graduate*, each year movies have grown darker, edgier, more morally ambiguous. The 77th Academy Awards winner, *Million Dollar Baby*, was an emotionally compelling film with an agenda revealed only at the end: the romanticizing of euthanasia.

On other fronts, recently acclaimed films *Cider House Rules* (1999) and *Vera Drake* (2004) have gone to great lengths to portray abortion sympathetically, with the abortionist as a heroic and noble figure.

Some films, like *Mystic River*, rise to the top of the critical heap without much of an agenda other than pushing darkness and despair.

More and more, it seems, modern filmmakers have much more than entertainment on their minds. In spite of the fact that family-friendly movies make the best money at box office, the powers that be continue to push a "sophisticated," amoral, and politically correct worldview in technically superb and seductive multisensory packages.

It may seem only reasonable for Christians to avoid their message altogether.

Then again, for some—especially those desiring to minister to those still walking in darkness—ignoring "bad" movies may be self-defeating. It's fair to say that the more we turn away from our own culture, the less equipped we are to take it on, to join in the spiritual battle for those whose souls are still in play. After all, God never censored wickedness and evil from Scripture but used it to show us the weakness of humanity and the wages of sin.

Those weaknesses and wages remain with us today.

I believe as he was speaking on Mars Hill, Paul truly cared about those he was going to witness to. Rather than carrying a sign saying, "God Hates Idolaters," he showed respect for them by demonstrating his understanding of where they were coming from.

I believe that if we truly love our neighbors, our

knowledge of what's going on in the secular arena of ideas gives us a place to start: "Yes, *Million Dollar Baby* was a powerful movie, but I'm not sure I can go along with the ending." Nor must we fear contamination from familiarizing ourselves with the things of this world in order to speak to others of the next.

RESOURCES

Movie reviews in your local paper may be written by someone with different sensibilities and different worldviews than you.

Reviews from a Christian perspective are available online at the following sites:

<www.movieguide.org>, informing and equipping viewers "to make wise media choices based on the biblical worldview."

<www.crosswalk.com/fun/movies>: ditto. Very reader-friendly and lively site.

<www.pluggedinonline.com>. *Focus on the Family's* site covers music (Christian and non-Christian), movies, and television shows that appeal specifically to teens.

Never assume because a certain movie is acceptable that its sequel will be. For example, while *Legally Blond* may have been tolerable, *Legally Blonde II*, under a different director and with a definite anti-Christian bias, was not.

Don't get me wrong. I'm not talking about willy-nilly consumption of stupid Austin Powers or *Dumb and Dumber* movies, but about making shrewd and selective choices, through reading reviews, about what popular books and movies might be great discussion-starters.

This is why I study movies. Even though most movies aren't acceptable for me to see, I pore over reviews and see a selected few (with the help of the fast-forward button on the remote). I analyze for worldviews and themes, propaganda tactics (as in *Cider House Rules, Vera Drake*, and *Million Dollar Baby*'s treatment of abortion and euthanasia as noble) and trends (one season's manifold portrayals of Satan, another's emphasis on reincarnation).

I study movies because Hollywood is one of the most important agents shaping the soul of our country. Films—with their unmatched visual impact—have proven themselves a powerful instrument in lowering standards and persuading people to accept practices once taboo—premarital sex, adultery, homosexuality, and abortion.

I study movies because I need to understand what makes my neighbor tick. I study movies because if I want to reach beyond the choir, if I want to compete in the realm of ideas, if I want to be salt and light, I must understand the postmodern mind in America.

Those who have grown up as Christians and remained true to their faith may find the postmodern worldview rather baffling. It helps to go back to the 1960s to trace the unrest that generated it. My own background is pretty illustrative of the forces that set it in motion and typical of the mind-set of today's liberal movers and shakers:

I just happened to be in the right place at the right time to catch the extraordinary wave of the counterculture: Washington, D.C., as the 1960s rolled into the 1970s.

I remember exactly when it started—my passion for politics. In 1966 I checked a book out of the library, a collection of essays against the Vietnam War. I don't know what led me to choose it, except perhaps a predisposition to question the status quo.

I devoured every word on the commuter bus I took each morning to my job as a service rep for AT&T, then spent the rest of the day arguing with my coworkers. It was a lonely battle, but that didn't stop me from being fierce—and probably quite obnoxious—about it.

As the antiwar movement began to grow and mobilize, I found a place where I was no longer alone. In October 1967 100,000 protesters converged on Washington, and about half marched to the Pentagon. Girls were sticking flowers into the gun barrels and trying to make the soldiers smile. You've probably seen the famous picture. The soldiers stood impassive, disciplined, ordered—everything we were not.

There was a sense of solidarity as all of us inclined to criticize our country began to gather regularly. In conforming nonconformity I advertised my anti-establishment attitude with my tattered jeans, bare feet, and even a few tattoos.

In the midst of this, I acquired a boyfriend willing to follow along with my political program, though he was never as serious about it as I. Somewhere along the line, we were introduced to marijuana and LSD. I didn't like pot, but I did like acid, and I did enough to learn to think way, way outside the box.

Questioning authority, overthrowing the status quo, was the rule of the day. I hadn't been brought up with a moral foundation, so I found myself thriving on flouting rules and causing a stir, making people uneasy. Jeff went along with it, but it never would have been his first choice. Years later, in a Father's Day tribute to him as the father of my first two girls, I wrote,

> Contentment hung about you like a baggy old sweater. You loved to hang out, have a good time, and make people laugh.
>
> I, on the other hand, had a lot of sharp edges. On a mission to save the world, I was forever analyzing, agitating, sounding an alarm.
>
> I didn't place much value on baggy old sweaters.

Still, in spite of our differences, we got married in 1968. I had grown up in a fatherless and troubled home. Part of me longed to build something stable and real. Jeff loved me and was kind. Now with that security, ironically, I felt even freer to spread my wings, continuing to show up for every demonstration—sometimes getting tear-gassed—and even getting involved in behind-the-scenes antiwar work.

Movement types were united by this overpowering feeling of "us vs. them." "Them" was the government, the police ("pigs" as I shamefully recall we called them), and anyone who stood for tradition or morality. By now we were no longer just antiwar but rabidly counterculture. Our paranoia was so great that we thought our phones were being tapped. We had begun to hate our government and all it stood for. Watching the first lunar landing in July 1969, some of us—the most radical—honestly thought it was being staged by those in power to impress the American public, giving them a false sense of patriotism and diverting attention from the war.

I was pregnant that summer, by August too pregnant to go to Woodstock, New York—much to my regret. On September 17, in the throes of labor, I waddled into Georgetown University Hospital with Jeff.

This was before sensible and compassionate childbirth. As usual, pursuing a different path, I had searched hard for the few-and-far-between books on natural childbirth and breastfeeding that were available then. To the hospital staff this meant simply no pain relief. Other than that, the experience was barbaric: I was strapped to a rigid table, wheeled into a delivery/operating room surrounded by people in masks, including Jeff—there only because of our take-no-prisoners approach to his being with me. After the baby was born, they took her away for 12 hours observation while I was not allowed to get out of bed even to go to the bathroom, much less to go down the hall to see her. Jeff had to leave at the close of visitors' hours at 8:30 P.M. All of this was standard procedure for births in 1969.

By the next morning, after an achingly sleepless night without my baby, I found my voice. When my doctor came to check me, I insisted on leaving immediately. Not a big deal today, but back then—well, my neighbors couldn't believe their eyes when they saw us coming home in less than 24 hours, when I should have been in the hospital four or five days.

I recount this for a reason. The counterculture was guilty of many mistakes, of implementing grand philosophical ideas that turned out to have disastrous consequences for the individual and society at large. Nevertheless, there were some good things that came of it. One was the reevaluation of the way babies were born in the United States. The counterculture movement was responsible for turning that process upside down, and today it is possible and probable that a baby will be born in a way that honors mother, father, baby, and the Creator as well.

So that was one good result from the counterculture movement. Another was my first daughter, Samantha Sunshine.

Now we were a threesome—Jeff, Samantha, and I. Samantha attended all the rallies and demonstrations in a front pack, then a backpack. My idealism—wanting to make a mark on the future—led me to want to become a teacher, and Jeff agreed to put me through college.

It was there that I made the evolution from antiwar activist to radical feminist—with some thanks due to Simone de Beauvoir's *The Second Sex,* which seemed to equate womanhood with imprisonment. Though I didn't feel quite that bad off, de Beauvoir's dissection of society and the secondary status of woman resonated with me. My work experience was all about male bosses and female workers. And ironically, counterculture men were no more egalitarian than the capitalists they reviled. To the guys in the antiwar movement, we were just "chicks." They hogged the microphone and never let us rally the crowds, just expecting the chicks to make coffee, copies, and love on demand. The Rolling Stones were singing "Under My Thumb." The sexual revolution seemed to have worked largely to men's advantage, removing much of the reason for even pretending they respected women as equals.

In addition, raising a daughter was alerting me to the cultural subtleties of sexism, like the lack of women role models. When I searched the library for picture books about girls for Samantha, there were just none to be found. It seems hard to believe since today there are so many, but it was a very real problem way back then. It wasn't as though girls were presented in a negative way—it was as though they didn't exist at all.

Eager to address all social inequities in my first child's upbringing—I had even bought Samantha a black baby doll—I spent hours with her storybooks changing pronouns from "he" to "she" and adding hair to male characters, human or animal. Picture the bird in *Are You My Mother?* with brown curls.

It's hard to fathom in today's egalitarian society—actually a society now skewed a little too much against men and boys—how little affirmation there was for girls and women before the Second Wave of Feminism. But it's important to recognize these roots and to acknowledge that something was amiss in the culture that needed to be addressed. And it's important to credit feminism—which with its rabid fixation on abortion has now become almost a caricature of itself—for the good it did accomplish in opening up opportunities for women, establishing equal pay for equal work, and allowing our daughters to enjoy the benefits of full inclusion in the culture.

The Second Wave feminists were angry, and in many ways they had reason to be. That the culture was male-dominated—making it difficult for girls to have role models and women to find outlets for their creativity—is a given. That there were double standards, justifying unequal pay for equal work as well as denying women with leadership ability the chance to use it, is also undeniable. Unless you're over 40, it's hard to imagine how much more difficult it was for women to become doctors or lawyers, to be published or recorded.

Without role models in the community and without encouragement in school, girls grew up without the options they have today. However, now I would argue that the pendulum has swung too far to the other extreme—producing a generation of girls brainwashed into giving up or postponing motherhood for careers, and producing a plethora of social ills.

GETTING REAL

The first fallout from feminism was the denigration of stay-at-home moms. After all, the proponents of "Take Your Daughter to Work Day" aren't thinking of having them stay home to cook and clean.

But working moms lead to daycare, and daycare is not necessarily good for children. According to the National Institutes of Health, children who spend most of their waking hours in daycare are three times more at risk for behavioral problems in kindergarten.

Their study—which followed 1,100 children in 10 cities in a variety of settings from care with relatives and nannies to preschool and large daycare centers—found a direct correlation between time in childcare and traits like aggression, defiance, and disobedience. These correlations were true regardless

of the type or quality of care, the sex of the child, the family's socioeconomic status, or the quality of mothering at home.

Jay Belsky, a principal investigator in the study, reported that children who spend more than 30 daycare hours a week "are more demanding, more noncompliant, and they are more aggressive."

Specifically, daycare kids "scored higher on things like getting in lots of fights, cruelty, bullying, meanness, as well as talking too much, demands that must be met immediately."[1]

Throughout history and cultures, parents have sacrificed to raise the next generation, but the Boomer generation turned this tradition on its head. *Father Knows Best* and *Leave It to Beaver* caused an almost visceral reaction among counterculture types. The generation that fought World War II came home to marry and buy a house in the 'burbs to "be fruitful and multiply," but a significant portion of my own generation decided against doing the same.

Perhaps if there had been no antiwar movement, there would have been no Second Wave. Yes, there would have been the voices of Betty Freidan calling the home a "comfortable concentration camp" and *Cosmopolitan* editor Helen Gurley Brown—who encouraged young working women to have affairs with married men—labeling the stay-at-home mom "a parasite, a dependent, a scrounger, a sponger, a bum."[2] But there would have been no cohesion among their readers.

The counterculture that arose united the hearts of anyone with a gripe about our culture or a predilection for selfish living. "Do your own thing" would be the basis for all the spin-off moral/cultural dilemmas that flowed out of it: abortion, reproductive technology, and euthanasia.

An important part of the mix was the sexual revolution, which really didn't start so much with the hippies—though they certainly ran with it—but with the introduction in 1953 of Hugh Hefner's *Playboy*, which strategically captured the hearts and minds of a large portion of American men. For some idea of its range of influence, consider that the November 1972 issue sold 7,161,561 copies,[3] while there were approximately 62 million males over 20 in the country.[4]

Even before "feminism" became a household word, we saw the serious seduction of a sizeable portion of American men who fell for the hedonistic, beautiful-women-and-lots-of-sex beckoning of an over-the-counter, not-hidden-in-a-seedy-adult-shop magazine—a magazine that published not only pictures of voluptuous naked women but also works by modern literary giants and interviews with very important men (including even born-again President Jimmy Carter), giving the whole package an air of respectability. The complexity of the package may have provided camouflage, but the theme delivered was plain and simple debauchery. Plenty of men did their best to emulate Hugh Hefner's glorified libertine life-style in whatever ways were available to them.

As far as *Playboy's* effect on women, this may have been the beginning of women's feeling that they would never measure up to the paper-doll ideal that over the coming decades would see woman's natural modesty broken down.[5]

My own father fancied himself a playboy and left my mother with three kids—only to start another family with a 10-years-younger wife. After four kids there, he moved on to an even younger wife. I guess we could call this franchise fatherhood. My mother, unprepared for single motherhood in the 1950s, latched on to one married man after another. I come from a long line of selfish people.

My parents, who split in 1954, were on the cutting edge of the rising divorce rate, but that was back in the days when one partner had to accuse another of wrongdoing. What really sent the divorce rate soaring was the 1975 no-fault divorce law. Once it took effect, 77 percent of divorces were filed by only one partner —and the incidence of divorce has quadrupled since 1960.[6]

My intent here is not to draw a pie chart with slices of responsibility divvied up among different forces that shook the foundations of the American family. Rather I would like to convey that while the Second Wave of Feminism can be pegged as a turning point in the history of the American family, and while it did indeed open a Pandora's box of cultural problems, the turn feminism took early on had already been pioneered by other forces.

As a feminist, I was largely motivated by a desire to make the world a better place for my daughter. And much of that has since been accomplished. Just a couple of examples: Women are no longer second-class citizens, invisible in the media and the arts. The medical profession has opened up, and now more women than men study to become doctors.

Yet when I steer my 12- and 15-year-old daughters through aisles full of provocative clothing in department stores, or when a television show I'm watching with my kids is interrupted by a Victoria's Secret commercial, or when aging feminists defend libertine politicians just because they support abortion-on-demand, I'm aghast at the large part of the early '70s feminist agenda that wasn't accomplished at all.

DIGGING DEEP

In the beginning, feminists were very concerned with the imbalance of power in male-female relationships. Their secular approach and measuring perspective saw womanhood as a type of slavery.

From the get-go, feminism was on a collision course with the sexual revolution. As the pill was supposedly giving women more

freedom, it was also making them more vulnerable to exploitation. Feminists simply shrugged and pretended that women could enjoy no-strings-attached sex. In their hearts all women know that isn't true.

But there was no attempt to deal with such subtleties, because for the majority of older feminists, the issue that early on became the number-one focus and that today seems to be the only issue that matters is abortion. Today's younger feminists seem to feel no discrepancy at all between expecting to be taken seriously in school and the workplace and dressing immodestly.

The early feminist movement could have gone in a different direction, thus changing the course of the culture.

Many of the early Second Wave feminists were motivated, as I was, by ideals of making the world a better place. In so many ways, they worked to better the condition of women.

That kind of sacrifice seems to be lacking in feminism since it turned a corner in its evolution—the corner where abortion became the defining issue. That issue brought out the worst in feminists. The bottom line of abortion was the taking of one individual's life to avoid inconveniencing another. And so the immense capacity of women for selflessness was short-circuited.

This new "me first" mentality became a signature attribute of the Boomer generation.

Yes, I know there were decent, hardworking people who were raising traditional families and doing well by their children, but they were not the movers and shakers of culture.

The movers and shakers were moving themselves into culture-shaping positions, such as university professors, public school teachers, newspaper reporters, and television anchors, anywhere there was influence to be had. Soon they were writing books and producing movies and television programs that reflected their new philosophy.

Virtually every media family for many years has been dysfunctional. Perhaps that's made the actual breakdown in the family that's been taking place seem OK by comparison.

And the family has been breaking down. Making fathers seem superfluous—plus the skyrocketing divorce rate and the faithlessness of many fathers—has brought us to a crisis with serious ramifications for children.

REACHING OUT

Despite the rosy picture painted for us in the media and diversity courses, growing up fatherless is just about the worst thing that can happen to a child. Check the statistics. They show children from fatherless homes are

- **4.6 times more likely to commit suicide**

- **6.6 times more likely to become teenage mothers**
- **24.3 times more likely to run away**
- **15.3 times more likely to have behavioral disorder**
- **10.8 times more likely to commit rape**
- **6.6 times more likely to drop out of school**
- **15.3 times more likely to end up in prison as teenagers.**

Fatherlessness is a reality of our culture. Yet single mothers and their children are usually overlooked and neglected—even within their own church families. The mothers need help and encouragement. The children need to spend time with intact families so they grow up with a vision to work toward.

As we look back, it's easy now to see that the Second Wave of Feminism was a major contributor to the breakdown of the family. Where it could have rallied for more respect for homemakers and mothers, it instead endeavored to convince us that women who chose this lifestyle were not living up to their potential. Thus they fell also into the trap of judging the traditional male role of breadwinner as superior to the traditional female role of making a home and caring for the family.

For members of National Organization for Women, who in the 1970s set the agenda for the women's movement, the traditional family was not a creative enterprise but a prison from which women needed to be freed. The pressure was on early feminists—and eventually on all women—to postpone or forego marriage and childbearing to pursue a "real" career.

The status of housewives and stay-at-home moms lost ground. Think of Hillary Clinton's comments: "I suppose I could have stayed home, baked cookies, and had teas, but what I decided was to fulfill my profession." That remark voiced the view of many professional career women toward professional moms.

Since feminists seemingly defined power only in terms of earning capacity, women were pushed into a position of envying men for their power in the outer world rather than sympathizing with men who lacked the natural power wielded by mothers in the home. As William Ross Wallace wrote in 1865, "The hand that rocks the cradle rules the world." Perhaps Wallace saw something profound that feminists have missed.

But the basic philosophical error of the Second Wave was that at some point it turned from idealistically seeking the good of all women to determining what is best for all women. And that was determined to be a career. Today many young women recognize that a mother's absence from the home comes at a price.

Dialogue is sorely needed now as we try to cope with the results of 30 years of moms being in the workforce and spending many hours each week absent from the home—an absence that has been anointed by the media as it sends the erroneous message women can "have it all." This kind of thinking promotes a selfishness that results in some women (and men) putting their own desires ahead of everything else, including the well-being of their children and even common sense. As we sort through these issues, we must be careful to remember that the majority of moms, regardless of whether they're pursuing a career or spending their days as full-time wives and mothers, have one thing in common: they love their children and seek to provide an environment that will give their children happy, healthy homes.

BUILDING BRIDGES

Discussion Aids

★ Give feminism its due. Acknowledge the beneficial effects of the women's movement.

★ Understand and be able to explain where you see the line drawn between benefits and harm—for example, women in the military.

★ Use the Socratic Method—asking questions that lead to the truth, for example, "Are a mother and caretaker completely interchangeable?"

★ Back your statements with facts, such as those on research on kids in daycare.

★ Acknowledge where men have fallen short in caring for their families, hardening women's hearts.

- ★ Be prepared to explain Eph. 5:22-33 not as a power relationship but as a template for mutual submission.
- ★ Search your heart for possible conformity to the culture. Replace it with respect for women who choose to stay home to care for their families.

Action Points

- ★ Clean up your own marriage of unhealthy power relationships. Live Eph. 5:22.
- ★ Use Bible studies for girls and boys to counteract the message that stay-at-home moms are somehow less worthy. Honor the concept of motherhood and fatherhood as goals more important than a career.
- ★ Organize practical help for single mothers and fatherless children. (One church I know sponsors babysitting, another free car care clinics.) In most churches, single mothers are at the bottom of the social hierarchy because they have little to offer, yet their needs are great. In the spirit of 1 Cor. 12:22, ask God how you may better serve them.
- ★ Befriend single-parent families. Invite them to dinner. Include them on family outings.
- ★ Welcome fatherless children into your home to plant a vision of how an intact family functions.

* Sponsor a Mothers of Preschoolers group as an outreach to socially isolated stay-at-home moms.
* Support organizations like Concerned Women for America and Eagle Forum.

SERVE YOUR COMMUNITY

59

When it comes down to basics, liberals and conservatives have more in common than either would probably believe. Way back when, Joni Mitchell sang, "I've looked at life from both sides now." I've actually lived my life from both sides—20 years on the left and almost 20 now as a conservative—and I feel qualified to say that both ends of the political spectrum are actually motivated by the same drive—to serve their fellow human beings.

It's just that members of each group—thinking inside their own established paradigms—have a hard time seeing this about the other side, because the ways of going about it are radically different.

While those on the right may view the politics and actions of the left as destructive, unraveling the moral fabric of society, aborting unwanted babies, undermining the institution of marriage, leftists view themselves as serving humanity by fighting to liberate men and women from the chains of tradition and hypocrisy. They have not understood that what they see as freedom others view as bondage. I know I didn't see it.

The passion is strong in those who lean left. They are driven by a basic belief that if they work hard enough, they can create a perfect world.

Keep these ideas in mind as you read more of my journey—first as a leftist through the politics of abortion and now as one finally discovering what it means to truly serve.

Even as a self-defined radical feminist, I still enjoyed my family. Jeff was supportive of my studies, never said no to anything I wanted, and changed diapers with the best of them. Every evening we took Samantha to the high school track, where she tooled around on her Big Wheel while Jeff and I ran a couple miles together. On the weekends we got together with friends, tie-dyed T-shirts, made candles, played Frisbee, visited museums, went camping, and dropped acid.

Just your typical hippie family.

My home life was far from oppressive. I was having too much fun to understand the angst other women were feeling, why Sylvia Plath would end up sticking her head in the oven, and why closer to home one of my best feminist friends would—on a regular basis—swallow a bunch of pills, only to be found by her husband and whisked to the emergency room to have her stomach pumped. Why were all these women so unhappy?

Sometimes it seemed the only credentials I had as a feminist were in my head. I read every new feminist book, argued with sexist professors, joined the National Organization for Women, but I desperately needed an issue to sink my teeth into.

And along came abortion.

When the Virginia legislature shut down our university newspaper for running abortion clinic ads, I came running. Although I had never needed an abortion myself—I had gone off the pill temporarily to have Samantha—all of a sudden advertising its availability became immensely important. What if something happened and the pill stopped working and I got pregnant and needed an abortion? How would I know where to get one if the school paper couldn't carry ads to let me know?

A small collection of campus rabble-rousers banded together, found *pro bono* lawyers, and mounted a class-action suit against the state for withholding information from students by withdrawing funding for the paper. Ironically, it was my wife-and-motherhood that won me the title of chief plaintiff. Who better to sound the alarm for anything having to do with "reproductive freedom" than a young and righteous student/mother with a toddler in daycare and a bright future looming before her—if only her life weren't ruined by another baby.

In those days I was thin and tan, with a long, curly shag haircut. Unlike a lot of the "Sisterhood is Powerful" crowd, with their clenched-fist-inside-the-women's-symbol logo and mentality, I was still smiling and approachable. So I was targeted for many newspaper interviews and serious discussions on television.

Had anyone told me then that 20 years later I would use the public speaking skills I learned in abortion advocacy for pro-life causes, I would never have believed it. Like many other feminists of the time, I was never able to agree to disagree. I hated those who stood in the way of abortion, period. And I don't use the word "hated" lightly. Just thinking of those who disagreed with my liberal politics was enough to evoke a visceral reaction.

Today I have become the person I hated so fiercely before. However, my experience has made it impossible for me to hate liberals. I know the fervor with which they cling to their beliefs. I understand that the desire to create a better world is the possibility that drives them.

My seizing the issue of abortion was a microcosmic example of what happened with feminism as a whole. The scattered nature of consciousness-raising groups and health collectives, all the writing and theorizing in the world, could not galvanize the Second Wave into an effective movement, a force to be reckoned with. Feminists needed a defining issue.

Perhaps that's why the "ideal" of abortion was

seized, as it seems in retrospect, with no questions asked. And yet in my research for this book, I found there were leftists from the get-go who found the idea of abortion not only repugnant but also completely contrary to the ideals of liberalism. Somehow they were silenced (though we'll hear their voices later in the chapter), completely ignored by the media who early on decided to frame abortion as a black-and-white, liberal-vs.-conservative issue.

Whereas every other group has been allowed to baptize itself, the pro-life movement, active from the beginning in trying to hold back the march to abortion "rights," was never called by its rightful name by the media.

From the first days of the Second Wave, feminists understood the power of language to shape predominant thought. Thus the crusade for gender-neutral pronouns and "Ms." instead of "Miss" or "Mrs." Thus the replacement of familiar words like "fireman" with "firefighter," "mailman" with "mail carrier," "spokesman" with "spokesperson."

And so, even before the term "politically correct" was coined, leftist women demanded certain terminology: "fetus" or "products of conception" rather than "baby," "terminated pregnancy" rather than "abortion," "pro-choice" rather than "pro-abortion," and "anti-choice" rather than "pro-life."

My own personal favorites are "family planning" rather than "birth control," and "reproductive rights" rather than "abortion." Think about it—those campaigning for reproductive rights are involved in the opposite—working to terminate as many pregnancies as possible. If that's not the truth, then why do today's feminists push legislation and litigation to ban the teaching of abstinence as a birth control option or to censor information given pregnant women that accurately describes the condition of the babies they're about to abort?

As I write, now back at home in Virginia (after the 30-year absence described in the introduction), our state assembly is headed for a showdown over a bill that would require some regulation of abortion clinics—which have for 31 years escaped any kind of health or safety oversight.[1] In Indiana a lawmaker has introduced legislation requiring high school health teachers to show students photographs of fetuses and teach them the health consequences of an abortion.[2]

But still, the left is chalking up plenty of victories: In New Hampshire a federal appeals court has just struck down new legislation requiring parental notification before an underage girl may undergo an abortion.[3] And California law provides that though they may not give a headachy student an aspirin, school personnel may take a girl off school grounds to obtain an abortion without parental consent.

Similar legal battles are being waged in states throughout the country, as abortion proponents resist any restrictions on "a woman's right to choose."

In the pro-life movement, I see the opposite. I see anti-abortionists supporting choice by working to make sure women know exactly what's at stake. Meanwhile, abortion proponents seek to censor information—and in the case of parental consent, to undermine relationships in which loved ones can support and encourage a healthy choice.

GETTING REAL

Abortion is not free of health risks. It is the fifth leading cause of maternal death in the United States—though many believe that figure is higher because abortion-related deaths are often not reported as such. In addition, a woman who has had just one abortion is at greater risk[4] for

- ★ **Breast cancer—risk is doubled after one abortion and further increased with more.[5]**
- ★ **Cervical, liver, and ovarian cancer.**
- ★ **Placentia previa in future pregnancies, jeopardizing her baby's health.**
- ★ **Ectopic pregnancy.**
- ★ **Pelvic inflammatory disease, endometriosis, chlamydia.**
- ★ **Future abortions—50 percent of women having abortions have already had one.**

★ **Emotional, behavioral problems such as depression, promiscuity, drug and alcohol abuse, and eating disorders.**

That pro-abortionists call themselves pro-choice only adds to the irony. Being pro-choice and caring about women and their rights would mean making sure they have all the information possible to make an informed choice.

And then there's the strategy all of us with strong feelings use from time to time of manipulating the language. There's a term for this: "doublespeak." It refers to language deliberately constructed to disguise its actual meaning. The word was derived from George Orwell's novel *1984*, in which the government used a practice called Newspeak, "deliberately constructed for political purposes: words, that is to say, which not only had in every case a political implication, but were intended to impose a desirable mental attitude upon the person using them."[6]

The most haunting example is certainly worthy of Orwell: In what are known in medical terms as "intrauterine cranial decompression abortions," a baby large and mature enough to survive outside its mother's womb is turned to breech position by the doctor, then pulled feet first down the birth canal until all but the head is delivered. The doctor then sticks a sharp object into the back of the infant's skull, inserts a vacuum tube, and sucks out the brains until the skull collapses, at which point the baby is delivered dead. Prolifers called this "partial birth abortion" and succeeded finally on November 6, 2003, having it banned as United States President George Bush signed legislation to make it illegal.

Throughout the battle over this procedure, the media have refused to call it "partial birth abortion," though it is a term used in medical dictionaries and Merriam Webster. You can find it at MedLine of the National Institutes of Health by doing a search on partial-birth abortion and finding these results:

Medical Dictionary

> One entry found for **partial-birth abortion**.
>
> Function: *noun* . . .
>
> An abortion in the second or third trimester of pregnancy in which the death of the fetus is induced after it has passed partway through the birth canal[7]

Still, the media refer to it as a "late-term procedure."

Three decades of media doublespeak has much to do with the acceptance of abortion as not quite the violent procedure it was originally recognized to be.

This whitewashing of the reality of abortion has produced a large population who, though squeamish at the idea, as in "I could never have one myself," still want to join the enlightened ranks by asserting in the next breath, "But I believe in a woman's right to choose."

The cliché of "I could never have one myself, but I believe in a woman's right to choose" diminishes the enormous weight of the subject and reduces it to a simple matter of preference, as in "Licorice? I hate it. But it's fine with me if others choose it."

Our society has been persuaded into believing that our feelings about abortion represent only prejudice and preference, not a response to a real and pressing moral concern.[8]

That's after 32 years of "a woman's right to choose" as law of the land—and we have indeed wandered far down that road. But let's back up to the months leading to Roe v. Wade, as the Second Wave of Feminism collectively, and I personally, were both defining who we were and what we stood for through the lightning rod issue of abortion.

Another force was also shaping the direction of feminism—the Sexual Revolution. While at first it may have appeared that the two movements, the counterculture's Sexual Revolution and feminism's Second Wave, were on a collision course, at some point they made peace with each other. Feminism, ignoring the very real differences between men's and women's sexuality, passed on the issue of women as sex objects and instead embraced complete sexual freedom.

This has led to incongruities such as some women dressing in a sexually provocative manner while blaming men for not taking them seriously.

It has led to soft-core pornography becoming mainstream. In the early days of the Second Wave, feminists would have regarded Victoria's Secret bra-studded women as exploited victims. Once feminism took a turn and yoked itself with the Sexual Revolution, abortion became the premier issue, and other concerns such as pornography and even child abuse became less important to the women's movement.

And really, the Second Wave of Feminism was never true to the ideals of the First Wave.

The First Wave feminists—the ones who championed and won voting rights for women at the turn of the century—were staunchly opposed to abortion. Susan B. Anthony in her publication *The Revolution* called abortion "child murder" and wrote,

> Guilty? Yes. No matter what the motive, love of ease, or a desire to save from suffering the unborn innocent, the woman is awfully guilty who commits the deed. It will burden her conscience in life, it will burden her soul in death; But oh, thrice guilty is he who drove her to the desperation which impelled her to the crime![9]

Elizabeth Cady Stanton referred to abortion as "infanticide." She likened it to slavery: "When we consider that women are treated as property, it is degrading to women that we should treat our children as property to be disposed of as we see fit."[10]

Victoria Woodhull, the first female presidential candidate and strong opponent of abortion, affirmed, "The rights of children as individuals begin while yet they remain the fetus."[11]

And finally Alice Paul, author of the original 1923

Equal Rights Amendment, is on record as saying, "Abortion is the ultimate exploitation of women."[12]

Second Wave feminists didn't agree. They saw abortion as a key to women being in control of their bodies and their lives.

The only problem was that not every state saw things that way. Prior to 1973, the reality was a legal patchwork, as each state had its own set of laws regarding abortion. In some, abortion was legal in all circumstances; in others it was limited in some ways; and in some it was never an option at all.

While in Virginia our class-action suit was percolating through the justice system, things were happening all over the nation—most importantly in Texas. There a poor, pregnant, and desperate young woman named Norma McCorvey was discovered by two young lawyers who had been looking for a plaintiff they could use to challenge the state law prohibiting abortion. Though Norma McCorvey was not exactly a poster child for feminism—uneducated, unskilled, addicted to drugs and alcohol—she became the "Roe" in Roe vs. Wade, the case that finally wound its way to the ultimate judicial authority in the land.

On January 22, 1973, the United States Supreme Court ruled that there is a constitutional right to privacy that covers a woman's choice about whether her unborn child will be born or not.

They further ruled that the state is not obligated to treat unborn babies—only they used the Latin term fetus—as persons, and that fetuses do not have the same rights as other human beings.

That was January 22, 1973, the day on which the future of the nation turned and began the slide down the slippery slope of moral relativism. When our culture no longer acknowledged God as the author of life but gave women that role, we began a moral freefall.

That turn has led us to a world in which

- ★ More than one quarter of babies conceived in the last 30 years have been aborted.
- ★ The womb is the least safe place for a baby to be.
- ★ Aborted babies are harvested—whole or in parts—for testing and transplanting.
- ★ Parents began aborting babies for such disabilities as spina bifida and Down syndrome but by 2004 were aborting for cleft palate and wrong gender.
- ★ Peter Singer, chair of Princeton's ethics department, preaches that parents of a child born with a disability should have 30 days to decide whether to allow him or her to live.
- ★ Planned Parenthood Federation of America (PPFA), in its 1998-99 fiscal year, claimed profits of $125.8 million on gross earnings of $660 million. Of the $660 million, $211 million came from clinic operations while the rest came from government funding and donations. And of the $211 million, $58.8 million came from abortions performed in Planned Parenthood clinics.

There's also the disquieting fact that one out of six women who have abortions—that's 250,000 per year—identify themselves as evangelical Christians.[13]

In many ways, this devaluing of children puts us out of sync with the rest of the world. Even in countries marked by poverty, parents consider having many children a form of wealth and a symbol of prestige. Money and inconvenience have nothing to do with it.

Were we to truly model the concept that children are blessings, perhaps fewer women would consider abortion a viable option for an unexpected pregnancy. At their desperate fork in the road, perhaps more mothers-to-be would choose life.

I hadn't heard that message, nor had I considered that way of thinking. Consequently, oblivious to the warnings of slippery slopes, I thought I was working to help the cause of women. All we wanted, I thought, was the right to terminate pregnancies so women wouldn't have to die from those "back alley abortions" the Sisterhood kept reminding us of. I was unaware of the value of human life.

So was Norma McCorvey, the original Roe. But after years of working in the service of the abortion movement, she became a believer. Now she works tirelessly through her ministry, Roe No More, to educate the public:

> For it is by knowing the truth that Norma was freed from the depression, drugs, and suicide attempts that accompanied her lifestyle as Jane Roe. Today Miss Norma, as she likes to be called,

devotes every waking minute to making known to the world that Jane Roe is in fact, Roe no more.[14]

Norma's story and my own are illustrative of the futility in arguing with abortion proponents. Believers who consider themselves pro-life need to understand one thing: Many nonbelievers have no way of grasping what you try to tell them because they have no concept of the sanctity of life. It was only through my acceptance of the Savior that the reality of abortion was illuminated for me. I also saw the many harmful places it's led us.

RESOURCES

There are thoughtful people on the left who are ardently pro-life. Listen to Mary Meehan, writing in *The Progressive* in 1980:

> **The abortion issue, more than most, illustrates the occasional tendency of the left to become so enthusiastic over what is called a "reform" that it forgets to think the issue through. It is ironic that so many on the left have done on abortion what the conservatives and Cold War liberals did on Vietnam: They marched off in the wrong direction, to fight the wrong war, against the wrong people.[15]**

In her lengthy article, well worth looking up and reading, along with many other pro-life liberal documents, she argues that

• The left has always defended the weak and helpless.
• The right to life "underlies and sustains every other right we have."
• Abortion is a civil rights issue:
Abortion exploits women
Abortion "is an escape from an obligation owed to another."
Abortion "brutalizes those who perform it, undergo it, pay for it, profit from it, and allow it to happen."

She concludes, "And the 'slippery slope' argument is right: people really do go from accepting abortion to accepting euthanasia. . . . We slip down the slope back to the jungle."[16]

The best we can do is appeal to conscience, to ask questions that may soften hard hearts—and to live our lives in a way that demonstrates we are truly devoted to the sanctity of life. As Charles Spurgeon said, "A man's life is always more forceful than his speech." By curbing our own selfishness and loving more sacrificially, we may have more impact than we would with hours of conversation.

And that's why we need to get involved in serving our communities. Service within the church—which keeps some believers so busy that their entire social life and social circle consists only of church activities and church friends—is safe and comfortable. It can make us feel useful and necessary, even when we're not. And it can insulate us from the real world—the fallen world, the world that needs our help. It can crowd out any opportunities to serve in a sacrificial and meaningful way, thus preventing us from fulfilling the legacy of Jesus.

WHAT DOES GOD'S WORD SAY?

"Jesus said to them, 'It is not the healthy who need a doctor, but the sick. I have not come to call the righteous, but sinners'" (Mark 2:17).

"You see, at just the right time, when we were still powerless, Christ died for the ungodly. Very rarely will anyone die for a righteous man, though for a good man someone might possibly dare to die. But God demonstrates his own love for us in this: While we were still sinners, Christ died for us" (Rom. 5:6-8).

Bottom line: Our true ministry is to those still very much a part of the fallen world and suffering the consequences of sin.

Shortly after I became a Christian, I came across the magazine "testimony"—a new word for me back then—of a woman who had been brought up in a Jewish home and then ran off to join the Hare Krishnas—those commune-dwelling, saffron-robed, tambourine-playing, deliriously chanting people who became known for selling roses at airports.

Her parents, anxious to undo the cult's brainwashing and allow their daughter to rethink her life, hired a professional deprogrammer. This guy really knew his stuff, and the deprogramming was successful and then some: it ended in a marriage in which God's hand was clearly involved, for during the birth of their second baby, Robin and Michael Strom became believers in Christ.

I was fascinated, as rarely did I hear of anyone who had made as radical a switch as I—and surprised to see in the byline that Robin lived in my county. I called and suggested we meet, then went to her house for a cup of tea. For 15 years now we've been good friends.

And for 15 years I've admired Robin's tireless service to her community, which began long before I even knew her.

In 1984 Robin was part of a group in Novato, California, praying to open a center that would provide pregnancy testing and counseling. With two abortions in her own background, this was an issue close to her heart.

By 1985, when the Pregnancy Resource Center finally opened, Robin's third baby had been born, and she was too busy being a mom to do much besides some post-abortion counseling in her home. But in 1990, with her children all in school, she began volunteering at the center. By 1994 she had become executive director.

The first major change she initiated was moving the center from its off-the-beaten-track location to downtown Novato. Robin prayed and pestered until she got the storefront she wanted—across the street from Planned Parenthood.

"I wanted girls who thought they were pregnant to really have a choice," she says.

"It turned out to be the week of the Pensacola bombing [a Florida abortion clinic] when we moved in," Strom recalls.

While under the shadow of the bombing others might have been defensive and standoffish, Robin thought outside the box: "We went to meet the Planned Parenthood staff right away, trying to defuse the situation.

"We prayed for them from the start and tried to maintain as good a relationship as possible. They had a prenatal clinic and sometimes sent their clients to us for clothes. Toward the end, they were even asking us to pray when their workers were ill."

In 1997, Novato Planned Parenthood received a directive from their headquarters to close—with only one week's notice. Inevitably, drop-ins increased at the Pregnancy Resource Center, and Robin realized that in addition to pregnancy testing and counseling, they needed to open a clinic to serve women who did choose life. It took two years, a major fund-raising effort, a move next door to a larger space, plus overcoming state, county, and city licensing hurdles.

The requirement of having a doctor on staff posed the most formidable challenge. Finding a Christian pro-life obstetrician-gynecologist in liberal northern California seemed an impossibility until Robin found Vickie Duncan, an African-American physician who had just moved with her husband and son from Bakersfield and established a practice 10 miles north.

Dr. Duncan, like many women of her generation, had never really objected to abortion—until 1982, when she was forced to perform them in medical school.

"I was performing a second-trimester abortion when the needle jerked suddenly," Duncan recalls. "I asked the head doctor what that was all about. He said it was the baby kicking the needle."

"It wasn't a spiritual thing at first, just a reaction in my gut that this was wrong. Later it solidified with my faith."

Duncan had to take a stand when interviewed for her current physician's group.

"When they asked me if I did abortions, I said no," she says. "So they asked what I would do with a patient who wanted one. I said I'd tell her to look in the Yellow Pages. Only one doctor in the group seemed to have a problem with that.

"But when I got this letter about the Pregnancy Resource Center position, my spirit almost leaped inside me. Two weeks before, our church had a missions conference, and I had prayed for God to use me. Now for the first time I understood that this was why He had brought us here from Bakersfield."

The Pregnancy Resource Center opened its brand-new clinic in September 2000, and since then Duncan has been overseeing the care of women who have chosen life.

"I can't tell you the satisfaction I feel knowing I'm part of an organization that rescues lives—even though I don't see the women until after the rescue itself," Duncan says. "The counselors are up-front with the mothers about the issues they will face. There's no sugarcoating. But they also help equip them to deal with problems."

So in her service to the community, Robin opened up opportunities for others to serve as well.

Almost from the beginning of her work with the center, Robin desired to go beyond treating the symptoms of sin—unwanted pregnancies, and not just among unmarried girls but their mothers as well—to deal with the roots of the problem. After an unsuccessful run for the Novato School Board (an unsurprising loss considering the anti-Christian atmosphere in Marin County), she put together an abstinence training package to counter the laissez-faire sex curriculum used in California, gathered another group of volunteers and trained them, then led them in taking an alternative message to Marin County teens—more opportunities for more Christians to serve.

Marin County, where only four percent of the populace attends church, does not take well to people with what they perceive as a morality-based message, even when it's based on just plain common sense—as abstinence is the only method that truly works to avoid not only unwanted pregnancies but also sexually transmitted disease. Robin has had to develop a thick skin and, as she says "a poker face" as she spends time in places where her views are misunderstood and her beliefs scorned.

For the past couple of years she has been attending monthly meetings of a collaborative of teen centers and clinics—including Planned Parenthood—aiming at opening teen clinics on high school campuses with the real agenda of birth control distribution—so kids can get what Planned Parenthood thinks kids need without even leaving campus—all the better for Mom and Dad never to know.

It's a difficult job, just being a silent witness—which Robin is right now—to all the group is planning to accomplish.

God has given Robin much responsibility, but He has also gifted her with leadership ability, and she has risen to the occasion. At times it has broken her heart to hold the secrets no one else knows—especially those concerning fellow believers, like the Christian mother who brought her teenage daughter in for a pregnancy test and then scheduled an abortion elsewhere to avert the humiliation of a pregnant teen in the family.

One thing is sure: none of her political opponents—who, remember, are convinced that they're serving their community through their efforts to provide safe sex for Novato's teens—can look at Robin and even begin to pretend she doesn't care.

Another woman whose early experience translated into community service is Tricia Goyer, a former teen mom and now the married mother of three who has recently written a book for teen moms called *Life Interrupted*. But her desire to help them goes back to 1999, when she also was involved in launching a Crisis Pregnancy Center in Kalispell, Montana.

"Right away we realized we needed to do more than just provide free pregnancy tests and counseling," Tricia says. "Choosing to carry one's child is just the beginning. I wanted to help moms be the best they could be."

In 2001 Tricia helped launch a Teen MOPS program—affiliated with Mothers of Preschoolers International. This group is known for its friendly way of coming alongside mothers and giving them encouragement and hope, something these often-confused teen moms need a triple dose of.

Just coming alongside and helping—what's so important is that Christians do this by simply serving, like the Salvation Army coming to Ground Zero in New York City not to evangelize but to meet the physical requirements of the workers daily facing the devastation.

When churches show the Super Bowl on a big screen and then interrupt halftime with a message about Jesus, that's not serving. And it's actually the kind of thing that completely turns nonbelievers off—just as anyone is turned off by bait-and-switch sales techniques.

Jesus is not a commodity to be sold but a Savior to be witnessed, not in the sense believers usually mean when they refer to telling someone about Jesus. We witness for Jesus when we serve without an agenda—whether in a Pregnancy Resource Center or a food bank or a hospital or a soup kitchen—out of love for our fellow human beings, not forgetting that we have all fallen short of the glory of God.

To be authentic, Christian service should usually be offered without an agenda. The action should speak for itself. Think of Jesus kneeling to wash His disciples' dirty, calloused feet. And remember these words of Francis of Assisi: "Preach the gospel at all times. When necessary, use words."

WHAT DOES GOD'S WORD SAY?

"Then the King will say to those on his right, 'Come, you who are blessed by my Father; take your inheritance, the kingdom prepared for you since the creation of the world. For I was hungry and you gave me something to eat, I was thirsty and you gave me something to drink, I was a stranger and you invit-

ed me in, I needed clothes and you clothed me, I was sick and you looked after me, I was in prison and you came to visit me.'

"Then the righteous will answer him, 'Lord, when did we see you hungry and feed you, or thirsty and give you something to drink? When did we see you a stranger and invite you in, or needing clothes and clothe you? When did we see you sick or in prison and go to visit you?'

"The King will reply, 'I tell you the truth, whatever you did for one of the least of these brothers of mine, you did for me'" (*Matt. 25:34-40*).

There are many ways to serve your community, and every Christian should go where God calls. I heartily recommend signing on with a nonchurch effort so you can at the same time rub elbows with nonbelievers and get to know one another.

Perhaps some of these suggestions may spark some interest:

- ★ Soup kitchens
- ★ Food banks
- ★ Disaster preparedness
- ★ Hospital volunteering
- ★ Services to the blind: training guide dogs and taping audio books
- ★ Easter Seals—working with kids with special needs

★ Babysitting for single mothers

★ Big Brothers and Big Sisters

★ Court-Appointed Special Advocates (this is an important niche that could benefit greatly from Christian involvement. (See <www.national-casa.org>.)

I chose to focus in this chapter on pro-life work to contrast the difference between serving with big grandiose plans for bettering society implemented through legislation and judicial review and serving with an approach the Christian community needs to become better at: individual risk, sacrifice, and service.

BUILDING BRIDGES

Discussion Aids

★ Study the issue, then share the truth about abortion and Planned Parenthood. Many people who think they're pro-choice have no idea how many abortions occur per year (1.5 million), that Planned Parenthood makes millions from abortions, or that viable babies (those mature enough to survive outside the womb) are aborted on a regular basis.

★ Use the Socratic approach. Ask questions: "When do you think life begins?" "Does the father have any claim on his child?" "Why do you think the younger generation is showing less support for abortion than the Boomers?"[17]

* ★ Be logically consistent. This means no exceptions for rape, incest, or the "health of the mother." (This is mostly a bogus issue—having to choose between the two lives is exceedingly rare.)
* ★ Share real-life stories of abortion survivors, like 27-year-old Fred Minnick (<http://www.seghea.com/emails/minnick.html>) and actor Jack Nicholson, quoted in the January 2004 issue of *Esquire*: "I would never want to vilify somebody who considered abortion murder. I was an illegitimate child myself. I may not have existed today."
* ★ Use surprise. Be familiar with liberal pro-life sentiments (see footnoted web sites).
* ★ Be confident but gracious. Never reflect feelings of rage such as those shown by pro-abortionists (who at their 2004 Washington, D.C., march bore signs saying, "Too bad Barbara Bush didn't have an abortion"). *In quietness and confidence shall be your strength.*

Action Points

* ★ Support your local Crisis Pregnancy Center. Take training to become a counselor, donate maternity and baby clothes, help raise money to purchase the newest 4D ultrasound machine. (<http://www.gehealthcare.com/rad/us/4d/virtual.html>), which shows moms their babies up close and personal.

★ If there is no Crisis Pregnancy Center in your community, consider starting one, banding together with other churches for a broad base of support. Contact Care Net (<http://www.care-net.org>) for training, support, legal advice.

★ Invite your local Crisis Pregnancy Center director to speak at your church.

★ Keep the Sanctity of Life a front-burner issue all year round—not just in January.

★ Start a post-abortion grief ministry. Urge women in your church to get honest about past abortions so they can authentically share with others from their own experience. (Google "post-abortion grief ministry.")

★ Consider adopting a child even if you are able to have more. If every Christian family adopted one child, what a world of difference we could make!

★ Invite a panel of adoptive parents to speak and answer questions. Encourage those in your church who would like to adopt but can't afford it to make their need known. Just as churches raise money for short-term and long-term missions, they can raise money to cover adoption fees. And what a wonderful way to share the spiritual responsibility for the adopted child—kind of a Christian twist on *It Takes a Village*.

FIND COMMON GROUND

Now that you've gotten to know me, it will probably come as no surprise that while television shows with titles like *The Bachelor* and *The Bachelorette* leave me cold, you can bet that one called *Amish in the City* would hold me captive each week.

In case you missed this cut-above reality show, the setup didn't involve gross-out stunts, eliminated contestants, or cash prizes. The territory to be explored was the consciences of 11 young people from two radically different walks of life: six hip, sophisticated city kids and five who had grown up Amish—in large rural families, typically without cars or electricity and completing their education at eighth grade.

The five Amish kids were imported from places like Ohio and Wisconsin to share a modern home in the Hollywood Hills with their urban counterparts.

Inspired by the Amish custom of *rumspringa*—a season in which Amish teens are allowed to explore the world and decide for themselves if they will commit permanently to the Amish way of life—the show was set up to entertain viewers with glimpses into the reactions of the Amish as they were introduced to the ways of the world.

Certainly it was a little contrived. And while it was intriguing to see the astonishment of the Amish kids on first seeing the ocean or being introduced to an African-American backyard family barbecue, it was somewhat painful to see how quickly the Amish girls embraced the clothing, music, and dance of their worldly housemates.

On the other hand, had the Amish kids not been willing to change, they might never have established any common ground at all.

One of the obvious set-ups was the inclusion of a very flamboyant homosexual. The producers must have figured he would serve as a lightning rod for the kids who had experienced little other than hard work on the farm, a basic education, and the Bible.

From the get-go, there was conflict. The Amish guys tended not to pick up after themselves; presumably because of their daily grind, the women at home cut them some slack. But the city kids were not at all given to sorting through cultural differences, just quick to blame. The city girls also complained that the Amish don't bathe enough, which may be simply because when big families live without electricity and have to pump their own water, something has to give.

In addition to the unwarranted antagonism of the city kids, Reese, the young gay man, certainly did his best to shock the Amish.

The Amish, hurt and bewildered by the cynicism of their city housemates, tended at first to retreat. Even though they came from different states and had never met each other, there was much common ground they shared—their family lifestyles, values, music, and the Bible.

On the other hand, the six city kids clashed not only with the Amish but with each other—over this one's extreme vegan beliefs (the root of all evil is meat) and that one's hypersensitivity to any perceived racism. The only common ground they seemed to share was the sense of superiority they felt when it came to the Amish, whom they considered unhip, uncool, and uninteresting.

If this sounds familiar, it's because it is. While the "religious right" stands on common ground when it comes to values, the "liberal left" is composed of a coalition of different interest groups with often-conflicting causes—for instance, what do predominantly Catholic pro-amnesty-for-illegal-immigration Hispanics and gay marriage activists have in common besides their determination to defeat those who don't agree with them on social issues?

In many episodes of *Amish in the City*, this same dynamic is evident as the Amish deal with "us-vs.-them" situations through quiet discussions based on their similar spiritual backgrounds and values, while the city kids are connected mainly by their contempt for the Amish.

The city kids also tended to prejudge the Amish. Because the Amish had been brought up with a perspective that considers homosexuality a sin, a belief they affirmed on the show, the city kids assumed the Amish would have a difficult time with Reese, the token gay guy. And indeed, Reese does his best vamping and preening in an effort to provoke them.

And yet with time spent together—on outings and simply living in the house—small breakthroughs occurred. It turned out that Reese alone had any meaningful selfless interest. Once a week he volunteered to work with mentally challenged children, and he invited the group to go with him. One of the city kids begged off, claiming he would feel awkward and this would not be good for the kids.

Reese's interest in and commitment to these kids revealed there was more to him than his superficial, flamboyant posing—and that he was more multidimensional than any other city kids on the program. Having assumed early on myself that Reese was a simple narcissist with little interest in others, I had to examine my own prejudices. Surely it resonated with the Amish that Reese was living out the mandate that all Christians share to care for "the least of these."

But the breakthroughs in finding common ground were pretty one-sided. The Amish were quick to embrace more modern clothing, try out new foods and entertainments, and even learn about other religions—through talks with a rabbi and an imam. But the city kids weren't interested in anything Amish, and when a trip was planned to visit Amish homes and help with the work of the farm, they acted completely offended and put upon.

Nevertheless, the Amish continued to extend themselves, leading to the most surprising situation of all. The 11 kids came home from an outing one day to be greeted by a surprise visitor: Reese's significant other, Eduardo. Mose, the oldest and natural leader of the Amish kids, welcomed Eduardo warmly, with no reservations, saying something about having heard so much about him and that since he meant so much to Reese, he was happy to finally get to meet him.

Later, Mose privately confided to the camera that he was not completely comfortable with the situation but felt it was the appropriate response for a believer.

Eduardo made a Mexican feast for everyone, and they all sat down to dig in. But Reese stopped them before the first bite, and in a trusting response to Mose's hearty welcome of Eduardo, Reese asked Mose to pray.

To me, this was a perfect portrait of Christianity in action. While there are many believers who dutifully intone, "Love the sinner, hate the sin"—and many who truly would like to, I wonder how many are still trying to figure out how to do it.

I think Mose knows how. He modeled it well: Go

forth and grab the sinner by the hand. Let him or her know how much you care. Then leave it all in God's hands and see what He'll do.

Like all homosexuals—and heterosexuals too—Reese is a wounded individual. To protect himself, he has created a defensive wall of cynicism, narcissism, and exhibitionism. He may have never met a Christian up close and personal. Just as many Christians stereotype gays, find their behavior revolting, and struggle with how to relate, Reese had probably stereotyped Christians, found their efforts to impose their morality revolting, and had no desire to relate.

And yet by making the first move to reach beyond their mutual prejudice and fear, with one simple gesture and a few kind words, Mose broke down the walls so that a real relationship could begin.

And now Reese is freed from his own cynicism. He can see the beautiful aspects of Mose's faith. He hushes everyone before dinner and asks Mose to pray. And then throughout the meal, he sings the praises of the Amish to Eduardo ("Edward-oh," as Spanish-language-challenged Mose continues to call him).

Perhaps Mose and Reese's relationship may not continue past the television series. But one hopes the old defenses and prejudices Reese felt toward believers will not be evident next time he meets a believer, and perhaps the tenuous relationship with members of the Body of Christ will continue, nurtured here by this one, there by that one.

We all must stand ready to be the next believer Reese meets.

But how do we prepare? If you're lacking up-close-and-personal experience with homosexual men and women, maybe mine will be instructive.

In 1972, after years of intense political activity, I was ready for a change, eager to explore the more recreational side of the counterculture. Like thousands of other counterculture types, Jeff and Samantha and I headed for San Francisco.

We moved into a small railroad flat in the Mission district, a mostly Hispanic neighborhood. From there, if you took the trolley in one direction, you could get off in Noe Valley, which was rapidly being renovated by young urban professionals, soon to be dubbed "yuppies." If you took it in the other direction, you would get off in the Castro District, the major meeting place for gay men in the city by the bay.

From the time I set eyes on it, I was intrigued by the Castro District. With my own bad girl streak, thumbing my nose at social acceptability, I was full of admiration for gay men who were so obviously and shockingly "in your face." The drag queens, the queer parades—they made it all look like so much fun. It was fun built on shocking others, making normal people squirm. We shared that in common.

During my first few years in San Francisco, I kept busy organizing an antirape group, taking a few radical classes at San Francisco State University, and finally having another baby—Jasmine Moondance, born in our bedroom at home while big sister Samantha collected admission fees from her friends on our front steps.

Shortly after Jasmine's birth, a fulltime drug dealer moved in next door and introduced Jeff and me to cocaine. I promptly fell in love with the drug and my supplier. Cocaine made me feel as if I could do anything or be anyone I wanted. Looking back, I think it made me delusional. I wanted to be a writer (though at the time I had nothing of any importance to say). But more than anything, I decided, I wanted to be free. Within a few months I left Jeff and Samantha—taking Jasmine and a few pieces of furniture to make my own way in the world.

Thus were the doors flung wide to a few years of promiscuity, small-time drug dealing, and adventures as a "fag hag," hanging out with gay men.

Oscar was the first gay man I knew well. He gave me my first haircut in San Francisco, and we became friends, trading gossip and giggles. After I left my family, he was there for anything I needed—from putting on a birthday party for two-year-old Jasmine to weighing out drugs for customers on my triple-beam scale. When I got sick and was hospitalized with pelvic inflammatory disease, he moved in and took care of everything, then stayed when I came home, cooking and cleaning and taking care of Jasmine.

Through him I met a slew of gay men. But I also met a lot through a group of artists and writers and poets I hung out with. And when I ran out of money and had to get a nine-to-five job at the phone company, there was a swarm of them there—guys who took drugs to get through a day of work to earn what they needed to party at night.

Eventually I came to spend all my time in their company, even had a couple more gay roommates as my life spiraled downhill through a series of drug dependencies. They were fun—and safe—for a single woman to be with. Plus, they were nonjudgmental about my own use of drugs and alcohol or my flings with straight guys.

Many of the gay men I knew had come to San Francisco from the Midwest or the east to get away from their families and live someplace where they felt they could be who they were.

I thought I was sexually liberated (translation: promiscuous), but these men talked about numbers of partners that staggered the imagination. This was pre-AIDS San Francisco, a city with scores of bathhouses and bars with back rooms providing the perfect setup for anonymous sex. At the time, the rate of venereal disease among gay men in the city was staggering, but episodes of gonorrhea were mere occupational hazards, and there were drugs to get over it.

Back then my own theory was that the sexuality of gay men represented the complete domination of masculine sexuality. Perhaps that sounds weird since gay men are often seen as effeminate—much of which may be affectations pieced together for a common cultural identity and a way of making the stereotypes their own.

What I mean is deeper. It has to do with the heart of male and female sexuality. Just as men often seem to be more interested in sex than relationship, and women put a greater value on relationship than sex, in San Francisco in the '70s gay men had virtually stripped sex of human attachment. They wanted sex without limits. And since women represented limits, they didn't want women.

On the other hand, lesbians are completely different: if you saw them cruising San Francisco's lesbian bars, you would think it was all about sex, but it's not. It's all about relationship and drama. Back in the '70s lesbians were much more likely than gay men to form couples. They were also the first to push out to the suburbs to make homes together. By 2001 Santa Rosa County, just 30 miles north of San Francisco, would be home to a large number of lesbian families—that is, two mommies and children. You would see them at PTA meetings and potlucks and parks and swim meets—wherever families were prone to gather.

But who knew in the '70s that homosexuality would become so normalized and accepted? Now it's clear to me that there were many more politically serious gays and lesbians than the ones I was hanging out with. Over time they gained positions of prominence in educational bureaucracies and corporations in California. Eventually they achieved positions of influence and power.

Meanwhile, my own life turned completely away from politics and the things of the world. As I detailed earlier, once I got sober and was free of the numbing effects of my addictions, I was confronted by the hole in my soul where God should have been. There followed a seven-year quest to find God, exploring every nook and cranny of the New Age movement, picking and choosing from a vast smorgasbord of spiritual beliefs and practices to put together my own religion. Early on I met and married a fellow spiritual seeker. Tripp became a second father to my girls. I say second father because Jeff, to his credit, remained very much a part of their lives, and by this time, following the 12 steps of AA, I had made amends for abandoning our marriage and the hurt I had caused.

Tripp and I meditated together daily and practiced prosperity thinking and affirmation to achieve our goals. By 1987 we had built a successful business, bought a home, and added three more boys to our family. This perfect picture was marred by one hidden problem: although we had been drawn together by our spiritual beliefs, thinking we were soul mates, Tripp and I were at odds about everything under the sun.

No wonder, since each of us thought we were the center of the universe.

Like *The Picture of Dorian Gray*, underneath the radiant, healthy image we projected was an ever-more-tortured portrait no one else saw. How surprised our friends—who flocked to us for spiritual advice—would have been had they known how on the brink of divorce we were!

But God intervened, and through a series of "accidents" we found ourselves at a Family Life Conference Weekend to Remember in San Francisco in March 1987. It was there we heard the Four Spiritual Laws,[1] a simple explanation of our need for Jesus and how we can receive Him. Written nearly 40 years ago by Bill Bright, the late founder of Campus Crusade for Christ, they have since introduced countless thousands to a true relationship with Jesus Christ. They are the last words Tripp and I heard before becoming believers.

In essence, we learned—

1. God loves you and has a wonderful plan for your life.

2. Humanity is sinful and separated from God. Therefore, a person cannot know and experience God's love and plan for his or her life.

3. Jesus Christ is God's only provision for humanity's sin. Through Him you can know and experience God's love and plan for your life.

4. We must individually receive Jesus Christ as Savior and Lord; then we can know and experience God's love and plan for our lives.

I had never heard anything like this before. Jesus was more than just another spiritual teacher! I prayed silently, confessing that I was a sinner and asking Jesus to become my Lord and Savior. Through my tears, I looked at Tripp. He was crying too.

We came home as different people. With no previous exposure to Christianity, we were not sure what had happened to us. But we knew something had changed.

Actually, it wasn't that *something* had changed. Rather, *everything* had changed.

In *The Weight and the Glory*, C. S. Lewis writes, "I believe in Christianity as I believe the sun has risen. Not only because I see it, but because I see everything by it." Certainly for Tripp and me, the world was now a different place.

Earlier spiritual concepts like pantheism, reincarnation, and personal divinity were immediately revealed as lies. When I say "immediately revealed," I mean as though a light had illuminated a place full of shadows: "Everything exposed by the light becomes visible, for it is light that makes everything visible. This is why it is said: 'Wake up, O sleeper, rise from the dead, And Christ will shine on you'" (Eph. 5:13-14).

And then there was the political realm. It was as though everything I had thought was true was false and everything I had thought was false was true. I was no longer a liberal, a feminist, or a moral relativist when it came to issues like abortion and homosexuality.

But I was also no longer a politically minded person. For the next 10 years I focused on being a follower of Christ. With no church background, I had little knowledge of the Bible at all and was learning stories about Noah, Moses, and Daniel, not to mention the history of Jesus, as I taught them to my children. My own learning curve was boosted by our decision to homeschool, which meant daily Bible lessons for the kids—and their biblically challenged mom.

Then there was American history, where I learned for the first time my country was built on a Christian foundation. It began to make me angry to realize how younger generations were growing up without this knowledge as so much vital information had been stripped from secular textbooks.

Revelation followed revelation. We had more children, including a son with Down syndrome, who changed our lives some more. (For that story, see my book *Lord, Please Meet Me in the Laundry Room: Heavenly Help for Earthly Moms.*)

In 1993 I wanted to write a book for homeschooling moms, and that led somewhere I never expected: to a career as a writer. For a number of years I studied my craft, wrote—and had published—hundreds of articles for Christian magazines. When I got a column in our local weekly, the *Novato Advance,* I began writing for the first time for a secular audience on family matters.

This happened to be during the Clinton scandals and impeachment. And I began to write about the impact on children and the family. My columns grew increasingly political, and I began to send them to other newspapers and national outlets like *The Washington Times*, *World*, and *World Net Daily*.

As mentioned earlier, in the summer of 2000 Focus on the Family hired me to write and edit the California state insert for *Citizen* magazine. Every month I did background research, investigated, interviewed, and came up with a reader-friendly rundown on some hot topic in the Golden State.

And were there ever hot topics!

While I covered issues like immigration, homelessness, abortion, cloning, evolution, more than half of my issues were focused on the ongoing struggle to hold back the tide of what seemed to have grown into an unstoppable force in California: the homosexual agenda.

It was like waking up Rip Van Winkle-style to find myself in a war zone. I just happened to be in the right place at the right time in the right position to report on the battles. The schools in my home counties of Marin and Sonoma were erupting with the results of 10 years of gay influence in the California education infrastructure.

With a liberal governor, two fulltime legislative branches with two-thirds liberal majorities (with a group of avowed lesbians and homosexuals holding key posts on important committees), and a solidly left-wing court system, those who supported only the traditional view of family hardly stood a fighting chance.

Not that they didn't try.

Californians made history in 2000 with their vote on a simple 14-word ballot proposition: *Only marriage between a man and a woman is valid or recognized in California.* Proposition 22, also known as the Defense of Marriage Act, passed overwhelmingly—61.4 percent for, 38.6 percent opposed—across the state. Of 58 counties in California, only four were opposed. No surprises there: Marin, San Francisco, Sonoma, and Santa Cruz.

Most would call this a mandate. But rather than feeling defeat, gay activists were challenged to work harder to achieve their goals. The public schools were where they really came out swinging, unveiling "diversity programs" with highlights such as—

- ★ School surveys to probe children's attitudes about homosexuality.
- ★ Integrating *all* curricula—even math and science—with pro-homosexual messages.
- ★ Relaxing gender segregation in locker room facilities, restrooms, and dress (so that a boy wanting to dress like a girl and use the girl's bathroom should be allowed to).
- ★ Posting "positive grade-level-appropriate visual images" that include "all sexual orientations and gender identities" throughout the school.

Many school districts had begun quietly sending teachers to Tools for Tolerance training at Los Angeles' Simon Wiesenthal Center Museum, where the holocaust is invoked and powerful speakers explore the topics of prejudice, genocide, hate crimes, and the role of police and educators. Just about every group—with the exception of Christians—is represented as the victim of oppression, including African-Americans, Hispanics, Jews, Muslims, senior citizens. And homosexuals too.

The Gay Liberation movement counts as its birthday June 27, 1969, when a routine New York police raid of Stonewall Inn, a mafia-owned bar catering to gay men, turned into a riot lasting several days.

This confrontation became known as the Stonewall Rebellion, and exactly one year later, thousands participated in the first Gay Pride marches in New York and Los Angeles.

In the ensuing years, gays have made enormous strides—filling television and movie screens with images of the gay roommate or best friend or wise neighbor. The new 2003 TV show *Queer Eye for the Straight Guy* was based on the idea that straight guys were lacking something, or many things, that only "queer guys" could help them with. Each week the Fab Five whipped some average Joe into shape with a crash course in grooming, interior design, wardrobe, and social graces.

I watched one episode in which they redid a dad by throwing all the kids' Fisher Price toys out of the house into the backyard, plucked his eyebrows, and dressed him in something sleek and chic.

The truth is, in spite of their self-portrayal as a

minority in need of special protection, homosexuals do not experience the same kind of discrimination as do racial minorities or people with disabilities. Their differences are based on behavior, not immutable characteristics like skin color. Certainly today they do not suffer economic deprivation or political powerlessness. In California gays now wield enormous power, at the state and many local levels controlling the curriculum content and classroom discussion, which now threatens to label as hate-mongers those who voice beliefs other than the new ones currently being embraced.

Besides advancing their agenda through the public schools, gay activists were mobilizing on other fronts to establish the right to gay marriage and to normalize gay adoption.

One method used to circumvent the public's opposition to gay marriage was to lobby for "domestic partnerships," which would grant same-sex couples the same legal rights as a husband and wife. In retrospect, this has proven to be not an end in itself but a means to eventually legalize same-sex marriage by advancing that agenda incrementally, just a little at a time.

But as it turned out, there was no "little at a time" in the push for gay marriage. In less than five years we were in the thick of it.

Vermont, a state that rivals California for the highest state percentage of same-sex heads of households, on April 26, 2000, passed laws establishing "domestic partnerships" and defining the package of benefits to go along with it: medical benefits, inheritance rights, joint state-tax filings, joint adoptions—everything granted to those who marry, except the word "marriage."

The state's web site labeled "The Vermont Guide to Civil Unions" notes that the law is not specific about the ceremony joining a man with a man or a woman with a woman in a domestic partnership and offers the following possible ceremony for civil unions performed by a justice of the peace, judge, or clergy:

> JUSTICE OF THE PEACE: We are here to join ___________ and ___________ in civil union. (Then to each in turn, giving names as appropriate) Will you, ___________, have ___________ to be united as one in your civil union?
>
> RESPONSE: I will.
>
> JUSTICE OF THE PEACE: (Then to each in turn, giving names as appropriate) Then repeat after me: "I, ___________, take you, ___________, to be my spouse in our civil union, to have and to hold from this day on, for better, for worse, for richer, for poorer, to love and to cherish forever."
>
> (Then, if rings are used, each in turn says, as the ring is put on) "With this ring I join with you in this our civil union."
>
> JUSTICE OF THE PEACE: By the power vested in me by the State of Vermont, I hereby join you in civil union.

Sounds a lot like a traditional marriage, doesn't it?

While California gays were writing education code and couples were unionizing in Vermont, the gay agenda was creeping along in the private sector as well. By 2004, 7,414 government employers were offering domestic-partner benefits.[2]

Still, there was dissatisfaction. And while conservatives disliked the semantic sleight-of-hand that granted gays all the benefits of marriage without the M-word, it was the M-word that seemed to matter most to gay activists. Not content to seek a parallel universe of privilege, they wanted not only equal benefits but also equal status. They wanted to tear down the wall that would still separate them from heterosexual couples.

Though Christian and pro-family groups have mobilized against the threat of gay marriage, it's important for you and me to recognize that this is a movement made up of individuals. Rather than simply defining this as a war between Christians and gays, and rather than painting the "other side" with a broad brush, ascribing to gays the worst possible motives—wanting to destroy families, America, and so on—I believe as Christians we are called to dig deeper for a more compassionate understanding of their point of view.

After all, as a member of the "religious right," I know how frustrating it is to be lumped into a category that identifies me as a hard-hearted, backward, joyless individual. That's not who I am at all. And my guess is that many gays are uncomfortable with the stereotype we hold of them.

RESOURCES

To bring yourself up to speed on news, or to find help for a loved one involved in the gay lifestyle, visit these sites for more information:
<www.family.org/cforum/fosi/homo sexuality>
<www.pureintimacy.org/gr/homosexuality>
<www.redeemedlives.org>
<www.desertstream.org>
<www.narth.com>
<www.exodus-interntional.org>

The fact is, while the scene in San Francisco may be much the same for today's young gay men as it was when I lived there—AIDS put a damper on things only for a short time—most homosexuals, like most heterosexuals, mature and change with the years, though many die too young to reach the wisdom of old age. (One 1998 *Psychological Reports* study, "Does Homosexual Activity Shorten Life?" reported the average life expectancy of homosexuals as 20 to 30 years less than of heterosexuals.[3])

It's worth noting also that lesbians don't suffer the same shortened lifespan, presumably because they tend to settle into more domestic lifestyles than homosexual men. Many more have custody of children and gravitate to the suburbs to bring them up in the best surroundings possible.

There are those of both genders who grow old, and often with a partner. They live quiet and productive lives as good neighbors and coworkers. Some don't have a political bone in their bodies or any desire to promote an agenda.

I know three such couples:

- ★ A pair of women who met in college in the '30s and have lived together in California ever since.
- ★ A pair of women with one biological daughter from a previous marriage and an assortment of at least half a dozen foster and adoptive children—all with special needs. They often take babies expected to die in their first year whose parents have given them up. They hold them and love them until they die. When I met them at Easter Seals after the birth of my son with Down syndrome in 1993, I couldn't help but notice how devoted they were to the children in their care and how they kept them nicely dressed, ferrying them to their many appointments with specialists. I was also struck by the fact that I didn't know any Christian couples sacrificing to this extent for "the least of these."
- ★ A pair of gentlemen in their 80s who bought a house in our neighborhood (in Virginia, not California!) and settled in rather peacefully to

take better care of their property than anyone for miles around. I took them a welcome basket. They come to see my children perform in school plays.

It's here the issue gets less comfortably black and white. When you let go of your stereotypes—the horrible excesses of Gay Pride parades and the in-your-face activists screeching—the real people God may put in your path should give you pause to think.

As I hope when they meet me and learn I'm a Christian, they'll have pause to think as well.

GETTING REAL

As the new teller typed in my transaction, my eyes graze his name tag, then the walls of his cubby—browsing for pictures of wife, girlfriend, kids, or pets.

Sure enough, there's a wedding picture, a couple under an arbor abloom with pink. Two tuxedos, no bouquet.

I wonder what he's thinking as he sifts through my bundle of checks—article payments from places like Focus on the Family, the Southern Baptist Convention, the Salvation Army. Will he pigeonhole me as his enemy? I'm not. I want to ask him how he got here, where he's going. I would really like him to know how much I care.

"You're new here, aren't you?" I begin.

"Are you from around here?" I smile a lot, maybe too much. I hope not.

As a conservative/Christian-come-lately, I've had to reconcile what I know firsthand to be wrong with the "other" side with what I observe to be wrong with my own. Here's what I see:

We claim to love the sinner and hate the sin, but the problem of homosexuality and its destructive effects within our society has surely made it a challenge. Still, it can't be right for Christianity to be pitted against homosexuality as though it were the worst sin on parade. I recently heard of a pastor who resigned his position and filed for divorce to marry the also-inconveniently-already-married church secretary. His main complaint: his wife was too fat. Is his sin less than Doug's? Such hypocrisy makes our very specific outrage over homosexuality difficult for those in darkness to understand.

As though it were planned, I seem to wind up with Doug as my teller more often than not these days. He sorts through my collection of "enemy" checks while we talk of the weather, the weekend, whatever.

It's not that hard. I know more than most that a life can be turned 180 degrees. In the meantime, I choose to be friends with Doug. Someday that may make a difference.

Andrew Sullivan is the kind of columnist you can't put labels on. That he's a liberal who was an early supporter of the current war on terror testifies to his ability to think outside the box. His comments are worth reading because they're authentic, not just following the party line. Mr. Sullivan also happens to be homosexual, and in articles available at his web site, "The Daily Dish," he has made an eloquent case for gay marriage as a boon not only for homosexuals but for society as a whole.

The most compelling was his February 14, 2004, column in *Time* magazine, "The M-Word: Why It Matters to Me," in which he traces his roots growing up in a conservative, middle-class Catholic family who valued marriage and family above everything, and whose parents successfully instilled this in their son:

> The most important day of your life was when you got married. It was on that day that all your friends and all your family got together to celebrate the most important thing in life: your happiness, your ability to make a new home, to form a new but connected family, to find love that puts everything else into perspective.[4]

Mr. Sullivan describes his loneliness as a teenager, not knowing why he wasn't like everyone else. Once he realized why he was different, it took him years to be honest with his family. And of course, they don't ask him the question they would ask if he were straight: "When are you going to get married?" That's a benchmark he's not entitled to look forward to.

Given the strong respect and yearning for marriage Mr. Sullivan was raised with, it may be not so surprising then that as an adult he still harbors that yearning:

> When people talk about "gay marriage," they miss the point. This isn't about gay marriage. It's about marriage. It's about family. It's about love. It isn't about religion. It's about civil marriage licenses—available to atheists as well as believers. These family values are not options for a happy and stable life. They are necessities. Putting gay relationships in some other category—civil unions, domestic partnerships, civil partnerships, whatever—may alleviate real human needs, but, by their very euphemism, by their very separateness, they actually build a wall between gay people and their own families. They put back the barrier many of us have spent a lifetime trying to erase.[5]

It doesn't help at all that Christians of all persuasions have not upheld the sanctity of marriage. A 2001 study by Barna Research Group showed the divorce rate for born-again believers was pretty much the same as for non-born-again subjects—33 percent to 34 percent.[6]

And how many pastors—even those in high and lofty places—have put years of antidivorce preaching behind them in order to sever their own marriage ties? Charles Stanley, pastor of the First Baptist Church of Atlanta and host of his "In Touch" television ministry, had been married more than 40 years when his relationship with his wife hit the rocks. On May 24, 2000, the Baptist Press reported,

> The Stanleys' troubled marriage was made public in the 1990s and caused some struggles in the church because of an unwritten policy that First Baptist not allow divorced men to serve as ministers or deacons.
>
> Stanley told the congregation in 1995, "If my wife divorces me, I would resign immediately."
>
> "We hate it that things like this happen, but our church is moving right along," said the vice chairman of the church's deacons, Jerry Beal, according to the *Atlanta Journal-Constitution*. "He is our pastor, and he will remain our pastor."[7]

Such things do not go unnoticed by those outside the Christian community.

Then there's the notorious January 3, 2004, surprise wedding of Britney Spears to her childhood sweetheart. After a romantic evening watching *Texas Chainsaw Massacre* in a Las Vegas hotel, they decided they wanted to do something "crazy." So they headed for an open-all-night quickie wedding chapel and tied the knot. Britney was wearing jeans, tee shirt, and a baseball cap.

The marriage lasted 55 hours. It ended in annulment.

For a lot of people, the same-sex marriage connection was instantaneous, producing a deluge of blogs and columns making the same point: why does the state deny sincere and sober homosexuals the right to marry—based on the tradition that marriage is a sacred bond between a man and a woman—while approving marriage for two reckless and shallow individuals?

It's certainly thought-provoking.

In 2003 the same-sex marriage ball really got rolling when the United States Supreme Court struck down 6-3 a Texas antisodomy law. Since 1960, when every state had laws against sodomy, 37 states had repealed those laws, and only 13 still had such laws on the books. With this ruling, all are now invalidated.

Justice Anthony Kennedy wrote for the court's majority: "The petitioners are entitled to respect for their private lives. The state cannot demean their existence or control their destiny by making their private sexual conduct a crime."[8]

Justice Antonin Scalia, joined by Justice Clarence Thomas and Justice William Rehnquist in his dissent, knew a slippery slope when he saw one.

He warned that "the court has largely signed on to the so-called homosexual agenda" and added, "Let me be clear that I have nothing against homosexuals, or any other group, promoting their agenda though normal democratic means." But, he noted,

> One of the benefits of leaving regulation of this matter to the people rather than to the courts is that the people, unlike judges, need not carry things to their logical conclusion. The people may

feel that their disapprobation of homosexual conduct is strong enough to disallow homosexual marriage, but not strong enough to criminalize private homosexual acts—and may legislate accordingly.[9]

Justice Scalia said he believed the ruling paved the way for homosexual marriages. "This reasoning leaves on shaky, pretty shaky, grounds state laws limiting marriage to opposite-sex couples," he wrote.[10]

Scalia was right.

On February 4, 2004, the Massachusetts Supreme Court, in a 4-3 ruling, ordered the state legislature to rewrite the state's marriage laws by May 17 to allow for same-sex marriage.

In an earlier ruling Chief Justice Margaret Marshall had written, "Marriage is a vital social institution. The exclusive commitment of two individuals to each other nurtures love and mutual support. It brings stability to our society." Now, explicitly precluding civil unions as an acceptable legislative option, she added, "The history of our nation has demonstrated that separate is seldom, if ever, equal."[11]

President Bush responded with this statement: "Marriage is a sacred institution between a man and a woman. Today's decision . . . violates this important principle. I will work with congressional leaders and others to do what is legally necessary to defend the sanctity of marriage." He stopped short of endorsing a constitutional amendment.

But eight days later and 3,000 miles away, the issue exploded when the mayor of San Francisco directed the county clerk to issue marriage licenses for same-sex couples. Between Friday, February 13, and Sunday, February 15, over 1,600 same-sex weddings were performed at City Hall.

Citing the need for a swift response as a safeguard against activist courts, on February 24 President Bush called for a constitutional amendment limiting marriage to the sacred bond between a man and a woman, saying,

> The union of a man and a woman is the most enduring human institution, honored and encouraged in all cultures and by every religious faith. Marriage cannot be severed from its cultural, religious, and natural roots without weakening the good influence of society.[12]

Rosie O'Donnell, calling Bush's words "vile and hateful"—rushed to San Francisco the next day to wed her partner of six years and other mother of their four children.

Activists say the weddings are a form of civil disobedience. They equate the illegal marriages to the civil disobedience techniques used by Martin Luther King to bring secure rights for an oppressed minority.

An unfounded comparison, according to Star Parker, an African-American former welfare mother, now conservative commentator:

> The gay movement is the civil rights movement turned on its head. When Martin Luther

King came to Washington and articulated his dream on the steps of the Lincoln Memorial, he spoke of an America that would live up to the truths and principles upon which it was founded. . . . The civil rights movement of the 1960s was about living up to and applying our principles, not re-writing or re-inventing them. There was no tradition on which this country was founded that Dr. King challenged. It was upon those very traditions that he made his challenge and claim. . . . Gay politics is the child of the new political America. In a fashion quite the opposite of Dr. King—who challenged an unjust nation to return to the principles and traditions from which it had strayed—gay political operatives work to re-write our traditions to suit their own proclivities. They say their struggle is about equality, but it's really about the exercise of political power and claims for entitlement.[13]

Should same-sex marriage prevail, it will be important for Christians to understand that even though the M-word is used, there is a distinction between civil marriages and those performed in the church. Perhaps we will be forced to render unto Caesar what is Caesar's and render unto God what is God's—in terms of individual people. There will be those for whom state-licensed marriage will be sufficient. But those belonging to God will continue to have church-sanctioned marriages.

I also think it will be important to stop blaming

homosexuals and accept our own responsibility for the decline in the sanctity of marriage.

Frederica Mathewes-Green, a writer on early Christian spirituality and cultural commentator, wrote on February 17, 2004,

> It's heteros who made marriage into a garbage dump. The ubiquity of soft porn, the 50% divorce rate, the sexualizing of little children, all of these have been destroying marriage for decades now, and it's not evil gays who did it. That we wake up and start shouting when some male couple asks for a marriage license is pathetic. Homosexuality does not pose a temptation to straights, that is, 98% of the population, yet the institution of marriage has been dying very efficiently without them. The loss of the label "marriage" as applying only to hetero couples is a very grave step and must be opposed, but in some ways it's like finally chiseling the date on a tombstone.[14]

As I write these final thoughts on same-sex marriage, I face at least a nine-month lag between delivering my manuscript to my publisher and seeing these thoughts in print. A lot can happen. But from today's perspective, I think gay marriage is something that is very likely to someday be legal in our post-Christian culture. Activist judges, a younger generation more tolerant of homosexuality than their elders, and the deterioration of marriage as an institution—all have led us here.

Then there's the issue of gay adoption.

In early February 2002 the American Academy of Pediatrics, a national organization with 55,000 members, threw its support behind second-parent adoptions for homosexual and lesbian couples.

In response, Capitol Resource Institute's Karen Holgate issued the following statement:

> There is a vast amount of research showing that homosexual relationships are not the best environments in which to raise children. On the contrary, children thrive in an intact family with both a father and a mother, and mothers and fathers serve different, but complementary, purposes in raising children. The AAP has caved in to political correctness and a political agenda—not the best interests of children.

The media has waxed enthusistic about normalizing gay parenting. On February 22, 2004, *20/20*'s Barbara Walters visited two dads with in-vitro/surrogate-mothered triplets, recording diaperings, feedings, and strolls—finally posing on the couch framed by the dads, a triplet in each set of arms. The message: *Barbara Walters says two dads are as American as apple pie!*

Homosexual men, unlike lesbians, rarely have the option of second-parent adoptions—which may be why 80 percent of homosexual couples seeking adoption are two men. Reacting to stalled homosexual adoption legislation in California, state representative Paul Koretz, who bills himself as an unwavering champion of the gay and lesbian community, said, "The battle may be over, but the war has only just begun."

In wars, innocent people are often wounded—a fact that seems to have escaped proponents of gay adoption who focus more on what they call "the fundamental right to be parents" than the welfare of the child.

Consider any same-sex couple desiring to create a "real" family. What would their adopted child miss? Nothing, according to the AAP, whose pro-gay-adoption statement citied research that homosexual households are no different than heterosexual when it comes to children. But the AAP ignored thousands of studies showing the superiority of traditional/mother/father households in securing a child's welfare.

We live in a nation where sacrificing our good for the good of others seems to be a more and more elusive commodity.

"Have it your way!" the famous slogan exhorts us. Birth control, casual sex, divorce, abortion, gay marriage, and gay adoption—all are on a continuum that began with the desire to take charge and have things our way. There is a thread flowing through these cultural phenomena—a refusal to accept God's design for marriage. Heterosexuals have rationalized their own violations of God's design rather than surrendering to a situation that would require them to lean more heavily on God.

When it comes to judging homosexuals, we

Christians need to be careful not to fall into the sin of self-righteousness described in Luke 18:9-14:

> To some who were confident of their own righteousness and looked down on everybody else, Jesus told this parable: "Two men went up to the temple to pray, one a Pharisee and the other a tax collector. The Pharisee stood up and prayed about himself: 'God, I thank you that I am not like other men—robbers, evildoers, adulterers—or even like this tax collector. I fast twice a week and give a tenth of all I get.'
>
> "But the tax collector stood at a distance. He would not even look up to heaven, but beat his breast and said, 'God, have mercy on me, a sinner.'
>
> "I tell you that this man, rather than the other, went home justified before God. For everyone who exalts himself will be humbled, and he who humbles himself will be exalted."

There are homosexuals who love God and try to follow him while holding on to their sexual lifestyle. Is this more wrong than women who have resorted to abortion or those who regularly indulge in adultery sitting every Sunday in our midst?

Taking a long, hard look at ourselves and where we've fallen short may be humbling, but that humility will make it easier to find common ground on which to meet our homosexual neighbors.

And we need to work hard to find that common ground.

A recent survey indicated that the kind of neighbor people least want next door would be a fundamentalist Christian.

How could this be? After all, aren't Christians honest, kind, thoughtful, compassionate? I guess at our best we are all that and more.

But sometimes, sadly, we're rigid, harsh, and judgmental. Too often our strongest opinions are based on things we know the least about, so that our response to certain books, movies, and television shows—*The Simpsons* comes to mind—is so exaggerated and off-base that we leave unbelievers scratching their heads in bewilderment.

Frequent conversations with nonbelievers will help us let go of our prejudice and fear and learn to see them the way God does. Why did that lesbian couple move out to the farthest limits of the suburbs? For the same reason you did—the school system's reputation promised the best education for their kids. Why did that long-term married-in-their-own-eyes homosexual couple move to the country? They wanted to retire in peace and quiet.

It's easy to define the world as Black/white, good guys/bad guys, saints/sinners, and to simply stick on the safe side. It's much more difficult to take some risks by getting out in the real world, making a personal investment in no-strings-attached friendship with people who are different, and engaging in real conversations—finding common ground.

In 1992 Bob Briner wrote the following words in *Roaring Lambs*, a must-read for every Christian writer, musician, and artist, as well as for those wrestling with the question of relating to our culture:

> We say we believe that God's Word relates to all of life and has the answers to all of life's questions. Yet we primarily spend our time and energies talking only to each other, writing only for each other, performing only for each other. This abdication has made it possible, even necessary, for evangelical Christians and their beliefs to be interpreted to the world primarily by non-Christians. The fact that they almost always get it wrong is our fault, not theirs.

How will they ever get it right if they don't know us? Yet how will they ever know us if we are so standoffish, so painstakingly different than they?

What are we so scared of?

I think of Jesus choosing fishermen—smelly, crude, maybe not so nice to be around—as his closest associates, or causing consternation among the "spiritual" folk by eating with tax collectors and prostitutes.

His commitment was obvious in His parables—to stand on common ground, to find ways to teach through the things with which His culture was familiar, to trust that the light within God's people is stronger than the darkness without.

I believe we can do that, too.

When I was a moral relativist, I had no problem

with homosexuality. When I became a Christian, I suddenly saw it differently, just as I suddenly had a different understanding of divorce or abortion or abandoning one's children. Rethinking my position on homosexuality—focusing on how God might like to see me behave—made a difference for me and my family. It helped us see that, no matter how passionately we oppose a political cause, we need to treat every person we meet with respect and kindness.

WHAT DOES GOD'S WORD SAY?

"All this is from God, who reconciled us to himself through Christ and gave us the ministry of reconciliation; that God was reconciling the world to himself in Christ, not counting men's sins against them. And he has committed to us the message of reconciliation. We are therefore Christ's ambassadors, as though God were making his appeal through us" (2 Cor. 5:18-20).

Two years ago I saw my bank teller Doug for the last time. Our family moved to Virginia, back to the old-fashioned values and traditions I had scorned in my younger, unbelieving years. Now we're in an even smaller town—so rural that our post office is a little cubbyhole in the back of our teensy, the-kind-you-see-only-in-movies general store.

On our tree-lined dirt road, graced with brick houses on three-acre lots, the house two lots down was recently bought by the couple in their 80s I mentioned before, who went to town fixing it up, with contractors swarming the property like locusts. When the dust settled, I brought over a welcome basket to the two men who had seen the same beauty in our neighborhood I had. Turns out they've been involved in theater all their lives and love to come to see my kids perform.

Where will our friendship go? I don't know. But I thank God for it, thank God for teaching me to love them, and—acknowledging my complete helplessness—I place all the unresolved issues into His care.

BUILDING BRIDGES

Discussion Aids

- ★ Study and be familiar with arguments—such as "born gay" or "one in 10"—pro and con. Know what homosexuals and lesbians think and how they justify their ideas.
- ★ Don't lose perspective: Does God hate homosexuality more than divorce?
- ★ Speak respectfully and with compassion, but don't soft-pedal your faith.
- ★ Share stories of healing.

Action Points

- ★ Never reject a friend or family member who "comes out" as a homosexual. Punishing through withdrawal of love will only confirm that Christians are hypocrites when we speak of love.
- ★ If homosexuality disgusts you, pray that God will fill your heart with His own unconditional love. Think of Mother Teresa ministering to lepers.
- ★ Minister to broken homosexuals through AIDS ministries or as a hospice volunteer, where, especially in urban areas, you'll probably meet AIDS patients.
- ★ Invite healed homosexuals to speak at your church. Allow time for questions and answers.
- ★ Designate a point person in your church—someone familiar enough with the issue of homosexuality and what it takes to leave it behind to minister to anyone who shows up needing help.

IMPROVE YOUR COMMUNICATION

They say a picture is worth a thousand words. But pictures are worth even more when it comes to saving babies' lives.

I'm speaking of the images captured by the General Electric 4D Ultrasound system, which debuted a few years ago with a not-a-dry-eye-in-the-house television ad:

In the background Roberta Flack singing, "The First Time Ever I Saw Your Face." A young woman's face reflecting anticipation, joy, amazement, gratitude. Her baby's face captured in 4D, the newest technology. The mother's face, now joined by the father's. The ultrasound image now in the background, with the technician moving the probe over the mom's pregnant belly. Close-up of the baby's face. The mother and father looking longingly and lovingly toward the screen. Roberta Flack still singing. Close-up of the baby's face. The mother's hand rest-

ing protectively on her belly and the father's enclosing hers. Wedding rings on both.

The voice-over says, *"When you see your baby for the first time on the new GE 4D ultrasound system, it really is a miracle."*

In the final shot, the mother and father are tenderly cradling their newborn baby. Roberta Flack is still singing.

When it comes to pro-life messages, it doesn't get much better than that. While GE may not have set out with the intention of making a pro-life statement in trying to sell their ultrasound machines, the truth comes through loud and clear: life is precious and wonderful and worth sacrificing for. With those ads running on television, there's no telling how many people who thought they were pro-choice experienced a subtle shift in opinion.

Crisis pregnancy centers nationwide were hip to the power of ultrasound before the advances in technology that made 4D possible. In spite of the expense of the machines (a used one runs about $20,000), many raised funds through donations to purchase one in order to offer pregnant women a "picture" of their unborn babies. Provided with the reality of the image, many women changed their minds about previously planned abortions.

Among the estimated 2,300 crisis pregnancy centers around the country, about 425 now have ultrasound machines—up from 170 in 2000. Crisis pregnancy centers are seeking government grants to purchase more machines.

The beauty of this type of persuasion is a positive message, grounded in love.

Now for the sake of contrast, let's consider another prominent pro-life organization and its campaign to confront people with the reality of abortion.

The Center for Bio-Ethical Reform, founded in 1990 and headed by Gregg Cunningham, also relies on powerful images to move people to choose life rather than death. According to their website, <www.cbrinfo.org>,

> Just as Dr. King sought to create a "creative tension" to awaken the nation to the horrible injustice of segregation, we too are creating a "creative tension" to awaken the nation to the horrible injustice of abortion.

And what tension they create! A fleet of trucks, covered with larger-than-life high-resolution photos of aborted babies with one simple word—CHOICE—rolls down the highway bearing witness to the goings on in abortion clinics all over America each day. The center also sponsors planes flying over California beaches and stadiums with 100- by 30-foot banners of aborted babies at 10 weeks gestation.

Their Genocide Awareness Project travels from campus to campus exhibiting graphic images comparing abortion to the Holocaust and other historical genocides.

Ironically, people seem to be more concerned about their sensibilities being offended viewing graphic images of aborted fetuses than they are concerned about abortion itself.

The center's aim is to confront Americans with the harsh reality of abortion. Even those who don't consider themselves "pro-choice" say things like "Well, I wouldn't have an abortion myself, but I wouldn't interfere with a woman's right to choose." (I'd really like to see politicians who were pro-life until it became expedient for them to become pro-choice stuck behind one of those trucks during rush hour!)

Yes, part of me is thrilled with the Center for Bio-Ethical Reform's strategy. But the sensible part of me, the part that responded to the invitation to surrender the rest of my life to Jesus, knows that this communication is not the kind that will win people over.

Consider a woman in a seemingly hopeless situation, considering abortion and stuck in traffic directly behind one of the center's trucks. She may feel more upset and guilty seeing the brutal reality of an aborted baby right in front of her. But guilt does not work to change people's hearts.

Take the same woman and have her accidentally stumble across the GE ad. I believe this approach stands a greater chance of turning her heart toward her baby. I believe igniting a spark of love for her unborn child can give a mom-to-be hope to conquer the obstacles she's facing.

So while prenatal sonograms and the Center for Bio-Ethical Reform's "Choice" campaign are both based on using visual images to show people the truth, their effectiveness is not the same.

And so the question is—what kind of communicator do you want to be?

Over the years, I've had regular column space in local papers in California and in Virginia. It was mostly about parenting, or the effect of current events or cultural trends on kids, mixed with a little family humor. Called appropriately, *Close to Home*. As I built a loyal following—even though I was living in a very anti-Christian community where only 4% attended church, I was able to bring up matters of faith and even use a Bible verse now and then. When readers trust you, they will cut you a little slack.

Because I spent many years hostile to Christianity myself, I was very sensitive to the things that might turn nonbelievers off. My goal when I used scripture was that no one throw down the paper in disgust, saying, "Oh, that Barbara Curtis is such a Bible-thumper! I'll never read her stuff again!"

Instead, I wanted readers to feel as I had when I finally got around to actually reading the Bible rather than just feeling contempt prior to investigation. I wanted them to be surprised and delighted: "I didn't know the Bible had such interesting things to say!"

You can see that I was careful. And things were going along swimmingly until the Clinton scandals erupted, at which time I began using my column to express loud and clear—and very cleverly, I thought—my displeasure with Bill and Hillary. Of course, in doing so, because I lived at the time in the most liberal county in the country, I alienated most of the faithful following I had developed.

I learned a lesson from that. As Goethe said, "Things which matter most must never be at the mercy of things which matter least." And I discovered that keeping the lines of communication open with the broadest range of readers was more important to me than my ability to skewer the political opposition.

That didn't mean I stopped commenting on political and cultural issues. For I believe what Martin Luther said is also true: "If a man doesn't speak to the issues of his day, he does not preach the gospel at all."

So the challenge for me became how to shine the light of truth on current events in as winsome a way as possible.

WHAT DOES GOD'S WORD SAY?

"In your hearts set apart Christ as Lord. Always be prepared to give an answer to everyone who asks you to give the reason for the hope that you have. But do this with gentleness and respect" (1 Pet. 3:15).

This verse became my columnist creed —and it can work for anyone who wants to

communicate more effectively. I broke it down into three words:

***Prepare,* but in your hearts set apart Christ as Lord. Always be prepared to give.**

***Share* an answer to everyone who asks you to give the reason for hope you have.**

***Care,* but do it with gentleness and respect.**

Barbara Johnson lost her first son in Vietnam, her second son to a drunk driver, and her third son disowned her because of his homosexuality. As a result, she has spent her life helping hurting parents laugh again. This tried-and-true woman has said, "Nobody cares how much you know until they know how much you care."

That's the secret of the best communication. Love bubbles up from it like fizzies in sparkling water, providing unexpected refreshment in what otherwise might have been rather uninspiring fare.

Especially when we communicate about controversial issues with those whose minds are already made up not to receive a word we say, the only power we can successfully appropriate that might have a slight chance of budging their closed hearts just slightly open would be a sense that we cared about individuals as individuals, not as members of one side or another.

The reason the GE ad works and the Center for

Bio-Ethical Reform campaign doesn't is because the former radiates love and wonder at the miracle of life while the second fixes blame.

Scripture says we are not to be conformed to the world. That means that even when we argue, even when we hash out disagreements with each other and with nonbelievers, our pattern should be different. Paul says we are called to be reconcilers. That means the burden is on us to be the more patient, the more careful, the more gracious in discussing controversial issues.

But God doesn't call the equipped—He equips the called. There are skills the believer can learn to improve communication with nonbelievers.

I worked hard at them while living in Marin County. I worked hard at them because I wasn't writing my conservative columns in an exceedingly liberal newspaper to stir up controversy or to prove how right I was or to scold. I was writing because I wanted to introduce readers to ideas they might never have heard before—ideas based on a Christian perspective.

And I do believe I succeeded.

The greatest compliment was when my husband—whose calling had him meeting hundreds of people a month in Marin County—would have a customer say, "Is that your wife who writes the columns for the newspaper?" Tripp might tense a little, because occasionally a reader would have something hostile to say—but only very, very occasionally. Most of the time the person would say, "I read her column every week. I never agree with what she says, but I love her writing."

And isn't that the point? *To be such an irresistible communicator that the other side feels drawn to continue the conversation.*

What are some ways we can do that?

Some of the basics are covered in the previous chapters. Briefly, let's see how they apply.

Increase Your Compassion

Christians often want to warn people Jonah-style of their wrongdoing and certain doom. We lack understanding of the bondage of sin and misread the motives of those fighting for rights believers know are wrong. We see the defiance, but we don't see the pain that brought the defiant one to that place. We forget that we were born with the sin nature just as they were. We forget that just as God loved us before we knew Him, God loves them too. We forget to see them through His eyes.

Once our hearts are flooded with compassion, there is no room for self-righteousness. Our voices change. We choose our words more carefully and show more respect. People can hear the difference. When they know we care, they are more inclined to listen.

Study Your Culture

At Little League games or swim meets, what are the other parents talking about? If they're all talking about the last installment of *Star Wars* or TV's *Family*

Guy or *The DaVinci Code*—and you're a Christian who's very careful to avoid worldly entertainment—you are missing opportunities to communicate and build relationships with those on your mission field. *Because each of us is on a mission field*. And for at least some of us that calls for a serious effort to understand the forces that shape our neighbors' worldviews.

Someone whose worldview is largely shaped by his or her entertainment—and who consequently believes in reincarnation or animism or same-sex marriage—may be able to hear best from someone who's seen the source of confusion and can talk it through.

Serve Your Community

A number of years ago we were living in a town called Petaluma (why the name I do not know!) when the town council decided to hear arguments on the issue of benefits for domestic partnerships for homosexual couples. The pastor of the church we were attending weighed in heavily on this. But when he urged us to attend the hearing, I felt sick at heart.

Why? Because probably no one in our church, including our pastor, had ever attended a town council meeting before.

And how does this come across to the town council members and other active members of our community? I'll tell you how it comes across: It reinforces the image that Christians are a bunch of judgmental high-and-mighties who are out to lunch until something comes up they want to come down hard on.

Would you listen to people who come across like that?

Christians should serve their communities because it's the right thing to do. But the side benefit is that in serving your community you earn the right to be part of the discussion about how it's to be run.

After Jonny was born with Down syndrome, we adopted another baby with Down syndrome. Twice since then we've been asked to adopt "just one more," and we've said yes. Though I had no other motive in adopting these special guys than providing a home for unwanted children, as it turned out I became a writer who frequently addresses pro-life issues. The results I've encountered are very reasonable: people can't easily write off my pro-life perspective when they see I'm involved on a daily basis and that it's more than just a political position or a bunch of words.

Find Common Ground

I had been a believer for only five years when Jonny was born, an event that really taught me to think outside the box. During those five years I led a pretty sheltered Christian existence as I was learning about the Bible and how to live the life of a believer. In contrast to the heavy involvement I had had with gays and lesbians before, I now had none.

But Jonny's birth opened the doors to a richer experience. One part of that richer experience was a couple I met at Easter Seals named Pat and Sandy, who had a couple of kids by one's previous marriage and a whole bunch of handicapped foster children no one else wanted. I was always impressed with how well-dressed and well-groomed the kids were—a good indication of the two mommies' priorities when it came to spending the foster care funds. Pat and Sandy also specialized in caring for babies who hadn't long to live and whose parents weren't up to the task—something I thought must be incredibly difficult. They spent many nights holding a dying baby through his or her final hours.

It was easy to find common ground with Pat and Sandy. We focused on our families. We cared about each other as parents of special-needs kids. When one of them told Tripp that if she had known there were men like him in the world she might have made different choices (they were pushing 50), as a victim of childhood sexual abuse myself, I understood where she was coming from.

Nowadays, with kids involved in theater, our family still rubs elbows with gay people. I refuse to be blinded by their homosexuality—and the political agenda that continues to confound and alienate believers—to the fact that they, like me, have sinned and fallen short and need God's grace. How will they see that if we don't show it?

RESOURCES

Even in my own relatively rural but rapidly growing community, the fallout from the

culture wars can be pretty surprising, including—

Public ridicule of parents who want sexually explicit library books removed from middle school libraries and of students complaining of dirty dancing at the prom.

Letters to the editor complaining about Boy Scout notices being sent home from public school (because the Boy Scouts will not accept gay leaders).

How did we get here? To understand the strings by which popular opinion was pulled from right to left, consider this definition from the Institute for Propaganda Analysis, an educational organization created in 1937:

> Propaganda is opinion expressed for the purpose of influencing actions of individuals or groups. . . . The propagandist tries to "put something across," good or bad . . . [and] seldom wants careful scrutiny and criticism. . . . The scientist, on the other hand, is always prepared and wants the most careful scrutiny and criticism of his facts and ideas.

The IPA lists seven basic propaganda devices, explained here with modern-day applications:

Name-Calling. People with questions are labeled "homophobes," as though they run on fear rather than reason. Gay activist organizations solicit funds to fight "religious conservatives," a stereotype that doesn't fit all their opposition.

Glittering Generalities. While name-calling leads followers to condemn without thinking, the glittering generality manipulates them to approve without examining the evidence. Words like "tolerance" and "diversity" become banners for those who refuse to practice these virtues themselves.

Euphemisms. Words and images can make unpleasant realities more palatable—as in "gay" for "homosexual."

Transfer. Gay activists have borrowed legitimacy by allying themselves with racial minorities, bypassing careful analysis of some very real distinctions.

Testimonial. Think Rosie O'Donnell, or any other popular gay celebrities.

Plain Folks. The two-mommy and two-daddy households of television documentaries and children's storybooks, like *Heather Has Two Mommies.*

Bandwagon. Presented with a paradigm of "tolerance" vs. "homophobia," many jump on the "tolerance" bandwagon without closely examining the real issues or the ramifications for the future.

Propagandists use emotions to push and pull, and they harness fear to steer attention away from real discussion and toward a quick solution—the one they want.

Take Off Your Church Lady Hat!

In California, English-speaking people often have the experience of walking into a store and hearing only Spanish being spoken by everyone else—customers and employees alike. If I were visiting Mexico, that's what I would expect. But in my homeland I expect to hear the language I was raised with and the language all my ancestors from Germany, Holland, Ireland, and Italy learned upon their arrival—English.

That's because they wanted to be included. Not trying to learn the language of the country you're living in shows a lack of desire to be included. I haven't moved or traded spaces—I'm in my own territory—but suddenly I'm out of the loop.

Not a good feeling. It goes all the way back to when I was little and excluded by neighborhood kids or snubbed by middle school cliques or shunned by the popular crowd in high school. People like to be included, not shut out.

Most Christians are probably not aware that sometimes the "language" they speak is almost as alien to nonbelievers as Spanish is to English-speakers. As someone who spent 37 years on the outside looking in, I can tell you that the clubby jargon Christians use leaves people feeling bothered and bewildered.

GETTING REAL

The following phrases are examples of the language referred to as *Christianese* or *Christianspeak*:

a word of prayer
blood of the Lamb
born again
Bride of Christ
brothers and sisters in Christ
church body
confess
covenant
demonic
feel convicted
found the Lord
have a burden
intercede
justified
ministry
mission
outreach
rebirth
reconcile
redeemed
repentance
saved
share (as in talking to)
sinner
stumbling block
surrendered
testimony
witness

You can read more at *On Mission:* "Unlearning the Lingo," located at <http://www.kintera.org/site/c.cnKHIPNuEoG/b.831001/k.FCF/Unlearning_the_Lingo.htm>.

Included wisdom:

"If you pray with a nonbeliever, be careful how often you address God by name in prayer. In normal speech you wouldn't continually repeat someone's name, but many Christians think it necessary to mention God's name after every five words or so. This is disconcerting to non-Christians. Above all, be real and be normal."

<http://www.kintera.org/site/c.cnKHIPNuEoG/b.829815/k.667A/When_Words_Get_in_the_Way.htm>

Included wisdom:

"People shy away from Christians

whose superior attitude and speech make it clear they view non-Christians as projects."

"Using the Right Words" <http://guide.gospelcom.net/resources/jargon.php>, with many useful resources linked.

Included wisdom:

"The test for every word, idea, concept should be: 'Will they understand this? This is for them, not for us.' Otherwise, non-Christians will quickly come to their own conclusion: 'This is for them, not for us.'"

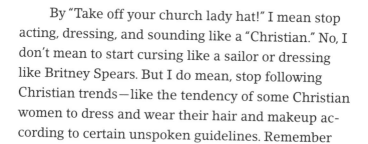

By "Take off your church lady hat!" I mean stop acting, dressing, and sounding like a "Christian." No, I don't mean to start cursing like a sailor or dressing like Britney Spears. But I do mean, stop following Christian trends—like the tendency of some Christian women to dress and wear their hair and makeup according to certain unspoken guidelines. Remember the year of the scarf?

Each believer knows he or she has an identity in Christ (Christian jargon). We don't need to prove anything to each other. We are not a gang or sorority or an organization that wears fezzes on our heads. We are individuals who can follow Christ while maintaining our individuality. Because we're all reflections of our Creator, like the facets of a diamond, that makes for a rich and vital group of people. And we can assume that nonbelievers will gravitate to different believers based on who they truly are as individuals.

So coming across as a member of a herd is counterproductive. It's not attractive, and it actually scares people away.

Focus on Principles, Not Personalities

Have you ever noticed that the media single out people like Jerry Falwell and James Dobson to put the scare into their readers about the "religious right"? The media have created a distorted image of each of these men, and they raise that image high when they want to provoke a certain reaction in their audience.

This is one example of focusing on personalities rather than principles. It's a cheap and easy way to manipulate an audience. Believers don't want to do that. We can stick to issues without using public figures as lightning rods to stir people up.

Another symptom of misplaced focus is ad hominem attacks, which believers run into frequently when they speak the truth. Sometimes in frustration, or because they don't know any better, political opponents will shift the argument from a discussion of ideas to name-calling and character-smearing.

Here's another no-no for those working on improving their communication skills: No matter how vicious your opponent becomes, don't follow suit. Simply hold up a mirror, then return to the facts: "I am not a woman-hater. What do you say we skip the ad hominem attacks and stick to the discussion? Now as to the number of secret abortions involving minors who may need protection from statutory rape laws . . ."

Keep in mind that you're discussing ideas, so—as my husband, Tripp, always teaches our kids—it's not *who's* right but *what's* right that matters.

Know Your Stuff

Whether it's homosexuality or abortion or euthanasia you care passionately about, whatever you plan to discuss, study and know as much as possible about the topic. Don't read only your side's take on the issue. Research and be familiar with the opposition. Try to walk a mile in your opponent's moccasins. Many homosexuals have been wounded as children, and that has prevented them from growing fully in their relationships with the opposite sex (although many would argue that this isn't true). Some really seem to have been born with a predilection for the same sex (just as some people are born with a predisposition to alcoholism). These are hard cases. But we limit our credibility when we know how to argue only in black-and-white terms such as *No one is born gay*. So many gays write or speak of growing up in confusion because they had no template for their same-sex attraction that it's not easy to dismiss this.

When you read something that resonates with your thoughts on a controversial subject—something written so well and so winsomely you think even those who disagree might be inclined to listen—cut it out, making sure to note the source and date, and save it in a file. Someday you may run into someone you would like to give a copy to.

Come Down from Your Ivory Tower

Even if you are one, do your best not to come across as a theologian, a preacher, or an academic type.

People hate being spoken down to. They like to feel comfortable and respected and accepted for who they are. They like to be addressed as equals.

It helps to remember that the ground is level at the foot of the Cross.

Jesus never condescended. Dwell on that a minute! He was the Son of God, and yet He communicated in a straightforward and accessible style that made crowds of people follow Him just in case He spoke again. Oh, if only we could keep people interested in the truth in even a small but similar way!

Jesus kept people's attention not by spouting off big philosophical or ethical treatises but by telling stories—stories of everyday life with everyday people experiencing everyday problems and finding everyday solutions. His language was simple and His metaphors familiar.

People don't need to be impressed by *you* but by *what you have to say*.

So keep it simple. As Eccles. 6:11 reminds us, "The more the words, the less the meaning, and how does that profit anyone?"

Know When to Wait, But When to Speak

As Scripture tells us, with not a wasted word,

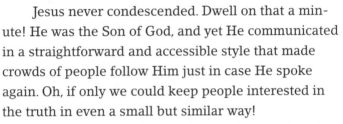

> There is a time for everything, and a season for every activity under heaven: a time to be born

> and a time to die, a time to plant and a time to uproot, a time to kill and a time to heal, a time to tear down and a time to build, a time to weep and a time to laugh, a time to mourn and a time to dance, a time to scatter stones and a time to gather them, a time to embrace and a time to refrain, a time to search and a time to give up, a time to keep and a time to throw away, a time to tear and a time to mend, a time to be silent and a time to speak (*Eccles. 3:1-7*).

Did your parents ever tell you that you were arguing for the sake of arguing? That was a pretty common thing for grown ups to say when I was growing up. And while I'm not sure I've ever said it to my kids, I know I've seen them do it.

Part of becoming a good communicator is learning when to be still and when to speak. If I have all my perfectly reasoned arguments lined up but blurt them out in my own self-will and not with regard to God's timing, they're likely to have no impact on the person I'm trying to move but will fly arrows so poorly aimed they miss not only the bull's-eye but also the tree.

Be Authentic

Good communicators stick to what they know. They're transparent. They share their experiences. They speak from the heart. They're not afraid to make themselves vulnerable—or maybe they *are* afraid but do it anyway for the sake of getting to the truth of things.

Someone once said, "If you bait the hook with

your heart, the fish will always bite." While you may not always be able to persuade others to your point of view, if you're kind and sincere, they'll more likely be drawn to rethink what you said later on. Remember—we're called to be Christ's ambassadors (2 Cor. 5:20).

Here are some additional things to remember:

- ★ Make eye contact.
- ★ Forget the stereotypes—see others as God sees them.
- ★ Listen carefully.
- ★ Acknowledge what was said:

  That's a good point . . .

  I hear what you're saying . . .

  I know what you mean . . .

  I've been there . . .

  A lot of people would agree, but have you considered . . . ?
- ★ Use the Socratic approach, asking questions that lead to the truth.
- ★ Share from your heart without thinking of winning or losing.
- ★ Be transparent and vulnerable.
- ★ If you don't know something, say so, offering to find more information.

Surprise people with humor or with a slightly different take than what they've come to expect from their stereotypical image of Christians.

BUILDING BRIDGES

Discussion Aids

- ★ The Prayer of St. Francis sets the standard by which Christians can evaluate their own communication:

  Lord, make me an instrument of your peace.
  Where there is hatred, let me sow love;
  where there is injury, pardon;
  where there is doubt, faith;
  where there is despair, hope;
  where there is darkness, light;
  where there is sadness, joy.
  O, Divine Master,
  grant that I may not so much seek to be consoled as to console; to be understood as to understand;
  to be loved as to love;
  For it is in giving that we receive;
  it is in pardoning that we are pardoned;
  and it is in dying that we are born to eternal life.

- ★ Even as we try to explain the truth about controversial issues, we must be dying to thoughts of winning and losing, to our selves and our pride, instead trusting completely in God to change minds and hearts.

Action Points

- ★ Be prepared to defend your position on the things that really matter.

- ★ Be prepared to let go of the things that don't really matter.
- ★ Know how to end a disagreement agreeably—agreeing to disagree.
- ★ Be bold and speak the truth—when the time is right to do so.

PREPARE FOR CONFRONTATION

I hear a sigh as I type the title of this chapter. Oh—it's me. I sigh as I remember the many times I've been compelled to stand up for a cause. I sigh because confronting problems isn't easy. I sigh because of the toll it takes on the Christian troublemaker—I mean activist—and his or her family. I sigh because if you're the kind of person who's compelled to speak the truth, to reveal wrong, to defend what's right, to render service where needed—then you have no choice. It's part of how God made you. Your only option is to develop a thick skin and learn to get better at your calling.

On the other hand, if you have seen problems and let them go, I want to challenge you to develop your confrontational skills, particularly if you know people who are out there trying to make a positive difference.

But be prepared. You may feel like the lone little Dutch boy sticking his finger in the hole in the dike, trying to hold back the tide that threatens the Judeo-Christian values in our increasingly secular society. Being a Christian activist can be a lonely calling.

That didn't surprise me when I lived in northern California. After all, I had moved there specifically to surround myself with like-minded radical leftists. Who knew that this counterculture chick, after years of being mainstream, would turn counterculture again—this time by becoming a born-again Christian and a conservative to boot?

For a few years all was quiet on the western front as I turned away from politics to learn the things I needed to learn about my faith. I didn't really plan it that way—I just see it in hindsight. And then I see that when the time was right, God directed my vision once again to the world I lived in.

I had come from a background that insisted "the personal is the political." I also knew it to be true that the political is the personal, that things that happened way up in the elevated circles of politics and culture had a trickle-down effect on families and individuals.

And so it seemed the most natural thing in the world for a mother with a lot of children at home—because by the early '90s I had nine—to begin addressing areas of political, cultural, spiritual, and domestic erosion.

I began a biweekly column in our local town weekly titled "Close to Home" and moved on to writing op-eds for our very liberal daily paper, the *Marin Inde-*

pendent Journal. There was plenty to write about, what with the Clinton scandals, the national epidemic of school shootings, and local skirmishes over things like Christmas carols in schools. Because of the makeup of our county, you can believe that my position was always the minority.

But I'm sure the newspaper management enjoyed carrying my column because it stirred up plenty of controversy.

I'm also sure I'll never forget the pain of reading the first hostile letters to the editor in response to my columns. It surprised me how much people could misunderstand what I said or attack me for things I had not said. In the beginning it hurt terribly, making me understand the expression "to lick one's wounds" in a very direct and cogent way.

And then, just as I was getting somewhat used to the whole idea of dealing with a little public flaming now and then, I unwittingly unleashed a veritable firestorm.

My son Josh was a sophomore in a prestigious Catholic high school in Marin. After homeschooling him in elementary school, my husband and I decided it was time for him to spread his wings, and we felt a private, religious high school promised a little more protected environment than a public school and certainly a good education.

It was one of those first gorgeous days of spring in 1999 when I stopped by the school for something or other, only to forget what brought me there due to my shock at the way the girls were dressed. Short, short skirts, halter tops, and lots of cleavage.

How boys could concentrate on schoolwork surrounded by so much skin was hard for me to understand. When I asked Josh about it later, he confessed it was pretty tough.

So I wrote a column for the paper comparing the girls' clothing to that of hookers I had seen on the other side of the bay.

What followed were three weeks of public castigation because I had broken some kind of cultural code by suggesting that females should think about the effect provocative clothing has on males and should opt for a little more modesty.

I do believe the paper broke records for the number of letters to the editor. I was compared to Hitler and to the Ayatollah. I was accused of protecting rapists. Most of the flack came from parents, surprisingly —parents defending the girls' right to dress however they wanted to.

Though my son was vice president of his class, he was immediately shunned. Slander about our family ran rampant. Things got surreal.

One girl wrote the newspaper that her mother had read my column and as a result they had fought over her clothing—and her mother had hit her. Hence, I was guilty of promoting child abuse.

To say that it was one of the most difficult periods

of my life would not quite describe the tension of living in a place where a large percentage of the population suddenly perceives you as a villain. And when you go out in public, you never know how many people wheeling carts around the grocery store are thinking mean thoughts about you.

To say it was one of the most difficult times, though, is not to say I'm not grateful it happened. I am.

I'm grateful because instead of spending the next five years gradually learning to deal with the fallout from my whistle-blowing, I was burned so badly that the scar tissue became part of the thick skin I would need for similar situations in the future.

And there were other things I learned.

Like how afraid people are to confront even the most obvious problems. I mean, with younger children at home, I really didn't go to the high school during school hours. But I know there were a lot of volunteer mothers who did. Why weren't *they* speaking up?

GETTING REAL

Be honest. How many times have you seen something going on you knew was wrong and didn't do anything about it at all?

If you really want to get real, make a list. Make a list of all the problems you didn't confront when you should have.

Think about what stood in your way. Ask yourself what God might have wanted.

Think about whether you'll be up to a challenge next time. Resolve to be obedient if God calls.

I knew there were plenty of people who felt the way I did because just as the paper was full of hate mail about me, my mailbox was full of fan mail—written by people who wanted to thank me for taking a stand—including male teachers who described how difficult it was to teach while looking at a room full of girls in skimpy skirts and parents who sent their children to a private high school for a good religious education but who felt constantly thwarted by those who didn't take their faith seriously but who wanted the prestige of an expensive private school.

Why don't you folks write letters to the editor about this? I wondered. I mean, for every dozen anti-Barbara letters, there might be one defending my position publicly. While I was grateful for the private "You go, girl!" mail, in public I remained pretty isolated.

But that's the point, isn't it? When someone takes a public stand for morality, those with a differing view may come down on that person swift and hard. He or she may become an example of what happens to those "right wing religious nuts who try to impose their values on everyone else."

And so for many of us, the farthest out we'll stick our necks is to write a private letter of support. That way only one person gets his or her head chopped off.

But in addition to learning how few people will actually take on the responsibility of confronting a problem—no matter how obvious—I also learned how few people are needed to effect change.

Because what happened was this: A conversation was started throughout Marin County about school dress—what was appropriate and what was not. The public schools even seized on the topic, and by the time the kids of Marin went back to school in September, almost every public school district had a dress code in place.

So in the end something happened I would have never dreamed possible when my pro-modesty column was published: adults took charge, and kids had to clean up their acts. And while I spent a few weeks feeling sliced and diced, in the end things changed, proving once again that the pen is mightier than the sword.

Over the next few years, with kids in private and public schools, I had to deal with other problems, not in writing but face-to-face.

When we moved from Marin to rural Sonoma County, California, we decided to put our elementary kids in the local public school, which in the country is the hub of social activities with good solid traditional families.

While it did not surprise me that the Christmas vacation was called Winter Break, it did startle me that at the Winter Program the children sang three Hanukkah songs, one Kwanzaa song—and not a single Christmas carol. This was despite the fact that out of the 150 K-5 students, there were no Black families, one Jewish family, and a pretty good number of church-going families.

Catching up with the principal afterward, I confronted the exclusion of Christmas thus:

"You know, I was surprised there were no Christmas carols at the program last night."

"What do you mean? The kids sang 'Up on the Housetop' and 'Jolly Old Saint Nicholas.'"

"But those aren't Christmas carols. Christmas carols talk about the birth of Jesus."

"Oh." She was looking at me like *And your point is?*

"Well, you know, the schools are all about inclusion and diversity. Christians are part of the mix. Our heritage needs to be represented too."

"Oh. Well, the music is up to the music teacher."

Next stop, music teacher, who being from California was absolutely ignorant of federal guidelines that actually encourage the inclusion of religious music in public schools.

That was not the end of the story, but the beginning.

In the seven years since then, Tripp or I have made appointments in October with any new music teachers our children have (with seven currently in public school, that covers several schools) to check out the music they are planning for the "Winter Program." We make the appointment well in advance, because we know they practice the music with the kids for a couple of months before performing it. If a teacher has no sacred music on the agenda, we give him or her a packet containing a copy of the federal guidelines to assure him or her that it's not only legal but also encouraged to include Christian pieces in public school music programs.

Once we've informed a teacher, we don't have to go back the next year. Actually the teacher is usually quite happy to find out that sacred music is legal, because as a music teacher he or she knows religious music is usually far superior to secular music anyway. As one Virginia high school teacher told his class, "When they start writing good Hanukkah music, I'll teach it. But not until then. I'm a music teacher."

RESOURCES

Charles Dickens in his classic *A Christmas Carol* created what must have been an unbelievable character way back when. As the quintessential Christmas enemy, Scrooge wishes that "every idiot who goes about with 'Merry Christmas' on his lips should be boiled with his own pudding and buried with a stake of holly through his heart."

Sounds a lot like our modern American Civil Liberties Union and some school bureaucracies!

Christians need to know that these folks are way out of line. Here are places to brush up on what's legal and get help if you need it:

Alliance Defense Fund: Christmas Project <www.alliancedefensefund.org/actions/currentactions/freedom.aspx?cid=3280>

The Rutherford Institute: Twelve Rules of Christmas <http://www.rutherford.org/resources/legal-12rules.asp>

While we expected to have issues in public school, we were surprised that our issues with parochial schools continued.

Although when we sent our four oldest sons to a second, more conservative, private high school, we expected affirmation of our family's strong pro-life position.

Boy, were we in for a surprise! One of the most popular teachers at school, whom we privately referred to as Comrade B. because of his socialist political views, spent 10 weeks in his social issues class on the death penalty. When I asked Comrade B. politely if he would be spending equal time on abortion, he said no, his reasoning being that some girls in the class might have had abortions and it would hurt their feelings.

Tripp and I asked for a conference with the principal and Comrade B., and as a result I was able to come and speak to each class about the sanctity of life.

When we moved to Virginia in 2002, I thought my days of school oversight would be over, but I was surprised when the first December we were here, Sophia told me her middle school resource teacher had asked the class to make holiday posters for the hallways but had forbidden them to use any religious symbols.

Of course, forbidding students such free expression is illegal. This was just another example of a teacher's unfounded fear. I wrote this article for our local paper, explaining the legal basis for students' religious expression in art:

Cut the Kibosh on Christmas Guidelines: Courts Back Students' Freedom of Religious Expression

My daughter's teacher gave this assignment: Make Christmas posters.

She also made it clear: No religion allowed.

I guess it wouldn't be Christmas without the fear of a lawsuit, would it? But this skittishness about religious expression in schools is unfounded. I know because I've been researching and reporting on this subject since 1998, when a couple of my kids were attending a small elementary school in dairy farm land an hour north of San Francisco.

My wake-up call came at the "Winter Program" where families sat through songs about Santa, chimneys, and reindeer, plus five Chanukah and one Kwanzaa—this though the school boasted only one Jewish family (nonpracticing) and not a single African-American.

Ninety musical minutes with nary a note about Jesus.

But while I have no fear that Christianity will survive whether censored out of public schools or not, that's not the issue.

The issue is the First Amendment. Are schools supposed to support freedom *from* religion or freedom *of* religion?

There's a big difference.

Which is why I share my California experience—it shows what can happen when schools become overzealous in their efforts to avoid promulgating a certain religion.

Because—let's face it—the religion we're always worried about not promulgating is Christianity.

It's this worry that leads some teachers to err on caution's side, nixing potential conflict by controlling the creativity and spontaneous expression of students.

I understand their dilemma. I really do.

But for those of faith—and I speak here of several faith traditions—this month marks a holy season. Some parents have worked hard to raise children whose faith is a vital, integral part of who they are as individuals—not just a label or a rote activity. If such parents have succeeded, teachers should not be surprised that what bubbles up creatively from their children reflects their faith rather than glittering generalities or superficial, materialistic aspects of the season.

This is a good thing—kids with convictions. And I promise not to be offended by your child's Menorah, if you promise not to be offended by my child's manger.

But we don't need to hash these things out on a case-by-case basis. The answers are already in place. Some years ago, President Clinton, concerned that some educators and community members had incorrectly assumed that schools must be religious-free zones, asked U. S. Secretary of Education Richard Riley to issue guidelines. The result is a remarkably concise, clear, and sensible document titled Religious Expression in Public Schools: a Statement of Principles (<http://www.ed.gov/Speeches/08-1995/religion.html>).

The guidelines affirm that while teachers may not encourage or join in students' religious activity, the school's official religious neutrality requires that:

"Teachers and administrators are also prohibited from discouraging activity because of its religious content, and from soliciting or encouraging antireligious activity."

The Virginia Board of Education is more specific. In the 1995 Guidelines Concerning Religious Activity in Public Schools, under "Student Assignments" it states:

"Student art projects often center around seasonal themes. Where the season has both secular and religious connotations, some students may prefer to depict a secular aspect of the season, while others may prefer to depict a religious aspect.

"So long as the expression is germane to the assignment, teachers should not discriminate against students who prefer a religious theme or viewpoint over a secular one (or vice versa). Example: Where different students depict a manger scene, a menorah and 'Frosty the Snowman,' the teacher may display them all on an equal basis, or on the basis of their artistic merit, but may not discriminate in favor or against any of them on the basis of the religiosity or secularity of their themes. Students have a right to express their religious values and viewpoints in their class work, assignments, and work products to the same degree that students may express secular viewpoints. A student's grade or evaluation must never be affected by his or her creed or religious belief or non-belief."

In addition to allowing student religious expression, the law is clear—on federal and state level as well as in courts—that teachers may teach in historical context the biblical origin of

Christmas, just as they may teach that Chanukah celebrates the victory of the Maccabees and the rededication of the Jerusalem Temple.

As for Christmas carols, not only have courts ruled consistently that they may be sung in public school programs, but teachers who neglect religious-themed music limit themselves and their students not only quantitatively but qualitatively. Carols, spiritual anthems, and choruses are among the most beautiful pieces of music ever written.

That is because the best art is inspired by that which we hold dear.

Dear teachers—because our children hold you dear as well—please honor the connection between creativity and faith, and do not dam the flow of your students' inspiration with barriers built from fear.

—*The Loudoun Times-Mirror,* December 18, 2002

While I could have gone in to see the teacher personally, since there is still so much confusion about what is allowed and what is not, I decided a public statement would be helpful. The fact that it's helpful is evidenced each winter when I receive reprint requests from parents and teachers for "that Christmas article you wrote a few years ago."

I include the article as an example of a typical op-ed you might want to write when there are problems to confront in your community. Just as anyone can send a letter to the editor, anyone can submit an op-ed to a newspaper. They're usually published on the page to the right of a newspaper's editorial page.

RESOURCES

Writing an Effective Op-Ed or Letter to the Editor

Make it short. 250 words for a letter, 750-1,000 words for an op-ed. Work hard to eliminate any extra words. A great book for learning this skill is William Zinsser's *On Writing Well.*

Edit yourself. Your piece will be considered by someone who's been writing and/or editing for many years. For your ideas and presentation to be respected, your piece must be free of grammatical and spelling errors.

Keep it simple. Use common, simple, straightforward language. Even when dealing with religious matters, avoid Christian jargon.

Use research or quotes from experts to support your ideas. It's easy for people to discount one person's opinion—not so easy when you back your opinion with experts.

Provide your contact information.

Call or e-mail to check your piece's status after 48 hours. Speak to the op-ed page editor. In smaller papers, that may be the top editor; in larger papers, it may be another designated editor. Ask if your letter or

op-ed was received and whether they plan to run it. If not, ask if there's anything you can do to make it publishable.

Understand your editor. **Be polite. Don't argue. Realize that this is the beginning of what may come to be a relationship. You may want to send another piece in a couple of weeks. If this becomes a regular calling for you, you'll develop a relationship with this editor. Even if he or she doesn't agree with you politically, the editor's job is to fill that page with interesting and thought-provoking stuff. If you can help with this task, he or she will come to welcome your submissions.**

Eventually, because I found there were so many things I had an opinion on, I secured a regular biweekly column space in my local weekly paper while still submitting pieces to our county daily every month or so.

If you're so inclined, having a regular presence in your local newspaper will give you the priceless opportunity of commenting on events—think Columbine, 9/11, Supreme Court decisions, Michael Jackson, Planned Parenthood fundraisers—as they occur.

When I moved from California to Virginia, though I couldn't secure a column here immediately, I sent in pieces that were published now and then until after a year a new editor decided to give me regular space.

That platform came in handy a few months later

when there was a specific problem I wanted to confront.

As the high school prom was approaching, I was very surprised that my sons—a junior and senior—did not want to attend. Under close questioning (well, I *am* a journalist of sorts), I found the reason why: the homecoming dance had been so lewd and inappropriate that not only did they not want to go to prom themselves, but they would not want to take a nice girl there.

"Where are the chaperones?" I wanted to know.

Apparently the chaperones—parents and teachers—had developed a habit over the years of turning a blind eye to what was known as "freak dancing." They stayed on the sidelines and remained nonconfrontational.

To say I was shocked is an understatement. After all, we had moved to Virginia from California in search of a more conservative environment for our kids. But what we were learning was that while most people here went to church, for many their faith seemed to be compartmentalized to Sunday morning and perhaps a meeting now and then.

While my kids were overjoyed when we first got here to find lots of Christians in their schools, they quickly learned that for many, church was another social stop and what they learned there had little impact on how they lived their lives in between.

However, there were a number of kids, like my sons, who felt the compromise of attending the dance was too much. They organized alternative activities—getting dressed up and going out to dinner, getting together at people's houses. One of my son's friends even organized an "ante-prom"—held the night before—with affordable tickets and a swing band.

I've written more extensively about this in my book *Dirty Dancing at the Prom and Other Challenges Christian Teens Face: How Parents Can Help.* But the point I want to make here is that my old confrontational bug would not let me rest until I wrote a column about the situation.

Because of past experience, I gave my editor a heads-up about what I was planning, and he suggested that I keep it generic—discuss the problem without specifically naming the school. I heartily recommend this kind of communication with your editor, by the way. His or her experience can often head off trouble,

In researching "freak dancing," I found that it was a nationwide problem and that many school districts had either banned school dances altogether or come up with guidelines to keep the dancing appropriate to a public school function.

Here is the column I wrote:

> **Time for a Fresh Look at Prom**
>
> Maybe it's time proms carry warning labels. As it is, most parents must be clueless about what goes on there.
>
> Curious when my own sons and many of their friends said they weren't going to prom, I

started asking questions. It seems that after one too many dances dominated by freak dancing—that is, groin-to-groin or groin-to-rear grinding once known as foreplay—they had just decided "Enough is enough."

A little research revealed that "freaking" has shut down dances in school districts across the country. Or forced school districts to forge written policies about what is appropriate behavior at school dances.

It's not just the kids who are to blame, but adults who dropped the ball in setting clear limits when freak dancing first reared its ugly head. Many parents would probably be shocked to see their normally well-mannered kids—who looked like Prince Charming and Cinderella in the pre-prom pictures—dancing exhibitionist-style a few hours later like an MTV nightmare (and parents who haven't blocked this channel are not doing their kids any favors).

See, the prom isn't like you and I remember it. It's a very dark room with hip-hop and rap music spewing obscenities and degrading stuff about women while kids get down and dirty.

Make no mistake: while some girls enjoy this kind of exhibitionism, there are many nice girls who are just giving in to peer pressure or pressure from their dates. Talk about buyer's remorse —I'll bet a lot of them feel pretty bad about themselves the next morning. Not to mention the growing number of prom-related rapes whose number seems to be growing each year.

Where are the chaperones? Good question. Loudoun requires one administrator, four teachers, and two parents at each dance. But remember, it's dark, dark, dark, and they can hang out on the sidelines, not seeing what they don't want to see. Besides, many are of the persuasion that "this is just what the kids are doing," "it's good for them to cut loose," "our parents didn't like the way we danced," etc.

I'm not buying this. Especially when even science is surprising us with new information about the immaturity of the teenage brain, with frontal lobes—the part responsible for decision-making—the last to develop, way after high school (<http://www.usaweekend.com/03_issues/030518/030518teenbrain.html>). While in calm situations, teenagers can rationalize as well as adults; under pressure or stress—especially that driven by hormones—they just can't cope.

That is why we need to still be involved in setting limits and guiding our children through these foundational years. Laissez-faire parenting might have been an option a generation ago, but I can't see it today. Not when our kids face a daily barrage of downright dangerous messages.

Don't get me wrong—it's a free country, and

> if some parents are cool with their kids freak dancing—well, throw them a party and let them grind away.
>
> But keep public school dances inclusive. Let this be the last year some of our best and brightest walk away from prom.
>
> —*The Loudoun Times-Mirror*, April 21, 2004

I also wrote letters to the principal of our high school. Then, when he didn't respond, I wrote to the school administration and school board.

The response was typical of what happens when you point out that something wrong is going on and needs to be dealt with. No matter how obvious it is, those responsible

- ★ insist there is no problem
- ★ circle the wagons against any further criticism
- ★ work furiously behind the scenes to fix the "nonexistent" problem
- ★ portray the whistleblower as a whacko
- ★ make the necessary changes
- ★ pretend nothing ever happened

It's definitely a frustrating process until you make peace with it.

In the dirty dancing saga, the prom went on with the customary inadequate chaperoning and inappropriate behavior. The following week, when a group of students banded together to ask for help from the school board in taming the dance scene, a cloud of media witnesses appeared, and dirty dancing hit the evening news. Believe it or not, there was a parent interviewed who defended the right of the students to "express themselves" through dancing, claiming any restrictions would be a violation of their First Amendment rights.

If you're called to confront problems, you're sure to find that there are those who oppose any calls for even a smidgeon of morality. It's something I can explain only with the scripture that says, "but men loved darkness instead of light because their deeds were evil" (John 3:19).

The school administration and school board never acknowledged there was a problem. In fact, they treated the pro-dirty dancing contingent of two students and a parent with more respect than the dozen students and parents who asked for their help.

However, behind the scenes, our $200,000+-a-year school superintendent called an emergency meeting of our county's 10 high school principals to discuss the "nonexistent" problem. They came up with a contract to be signed by everyone attending public school dances—as well as their parents.

And because our local school's prom was the first in the area, every other school used the contract for proms that spring. It's still in use today.

Meanwhile, I knew that people were very angry at me for "ruining the reputation of our high school." For a few weeks I was too uncomfortable to go grocery shopping, not knowing who was mad at me and who was not.

So when I say it's a frustrating process until you make peace with it, I mean this: We confrontational types see a change was needed, we do our part, and we see the change take place. What's missing is that we not only don't get credit—we get blamed. And that's the way it is. I made peace with it when I saw that God used me to accomplish things and that accomplishing them was all that mattered.

WHAT DOES GOD'S WORD SAY?

"Blessed are those who are persecuted because of righteousness, for theirs is the kingdom of heaven. Blessed are you when people insult you, persecute you and falsely say all kinds of evil against you because of me. Rejoice and be glad, because great is your reward in heaven, for in the same way they persecuted the prophets who were before you" (Matt. 5:10-12).

These examples may seem pretty small potatoes, I know, when you consider there are brave believers out there in higher places than I taking bigger risks and confronting greater problems. I offer my own personal stories as an encouragement to those of you who see our country's values steadily eroding away as a way of showing that there's a place for anyone to get involved.

The people I could not understand in my newly-adopted sweet Virginia homeland were the stalwart Christians with kids in public school who never took a stand to reclaim the territory of school dances for their kids. One family I knew with two daughters graduated and several on their way up through the public school system had heard from their girls what was going on but overlooked it. When I raised a fuss, the second daughter told my son, "She'll never change anything."

Where does that defeatist thinking come from? If an army was invading our country, would we just lay down our arms and let it happen? Then why let our morality and traditions and just plain good manners be stamped out?

Among the first people I met when we moved to Virginia was a very wealthy woman with a thriving business and family, including a couple of children who had graduated and several more still in public school. Because she was friends with the principal of the high school, who insisted there was no problem, she was skeptical of my claims about the dances.

The following fall, I challenged her to chaperone at the homecoming dance. When my daughter threw the challenge back at me, asking why I hadn't signed up to chaperone myself, I explained that because I was a relative newcomer to the community and still experiencing the fallout from allegedly tarnishing our school's good name, my presence would be a lightning rod, inviting bad behavior.

However, my friend was a high-profile woman with an established reputation in the community. Having come from a position like that in California, I knew from experience that a Christian so blessed should definitely be willing to take on more responsibility. So I reminded her that she could use her position to serve not just in her church but also in her community. Besides, as someone who had taught many of these kids in Sunday School, Vacation Bible School, and parachurch activities, I guessed that her presence alone would lift the behavior out of the gutter.

I guessed wrong. My friend spent the evening working hard to break up couples simulating sex on the dance floor, admonishing the deejay to play something other than rap, and reminding the principal whose word she had taken over mine of what was acceptable and what was not.

Perhaps the only good that came out of it was that she saw I wasn't making this stuff up.

Afterward, she said, "Barbara, you know my daughters told me about the dances. But you have to see it. It is so much worse than I ever could have imagined."

How in a predominantly Christian community had this happened? Because the believers with kids in public school had abdicated their responsibility.

Wherever you are, God calls you to rise to your maximum influence in the culture.

First of all, if you have leadership ability, if you

are gifted in analysis and can spot problems, too, then you have been given 10 talents. The Master does not want them buried in the ground. He wants to see them grow and flourish. Start confronting those problems you see, remembering to use the principles we've discussed. But no matter how carefully you use them, no matter how tactfully, don't be surprised to find that it's not the kind of job where people come up and grab your hands and say, "Wow—you did a great job handling that! Thanks!"

Just know that God sees and is pleased.

If you've been blessed with a position of status and influence in the community, remember that those things are yours only through the generosity of the Creator and that you have a responsibility to use them as leverage to accomplish greater good. If you're new to using your influence outside church circles, believe me—it works just as well in the world as it does in church.

One of the ways God has gotten me to go along with His plans is the fact that I'm an optimist and thus don't generally think ahead and imagine the negative consequences to come from whatever it is I feel called to do. That's an advantage. So if you do feel a nudge to tackle some problem, try not to imagine the fallout that may result, but instead stay focused on what it is you need to do.

And know that no matter what happens, God will see you through. Time has a way of smoothing any ruffled feathers. Nothing ever comes to stay, but as the Bible says, "It came to pass."

And one person's voice can be very important.

BUILDING BRIDGES

Discussion Aids

- ★ If you have children in public schools, sit down for a serious discussion about what's really going on. If you've not opted them out of sex ed, find out what's being discussed there. What about American history? Are their teachers respectful to those expressing a Christian point of view?
- ★ Are there times and places where freedom of expression should be moderated?
- ★ What factors make Christians—and make you—reluctant to speak up about problems?
- ★ Can the Judeo-Christian ethic prevail without strong defenders?

Action Points

- ★ Form a community involvement/political discussion group to monitor what's going on in your community and in the world at large. Share ideas about problems you wish to confront, brainstorm, and get support from others for.
- ★ Find ways to let your voice be heard that work for your time and lifestyle. (My daughter is a

busy homeschooling mom of five, so she participates via <www.onemillionmoms.com>.)

★ Know the names and e-mail addresses of all your political representatives—from the federal to the local level. Let them know how you want to be represented on issues.

★ Once you feel a nudge to do something, do it. Don't put it off.

★ Keep up-to-the-minute on those issues that resonate with you.

★ Consider joining a group like Eagle Forum, Alliance Defense Fund, Million Moms, or Concerned Women of America and subscribing to their e-mail newsletter to keep up-to-speed on what's going on.

TRUST YOUR CREATOR

Trusting God should be the easiest part. But I know for many of us it's not. It's something we're always working on.

Someone wrote me last week about Eph. 5:21-33, the scripture that has to do with wives submitting to their husbands.

She asked, "Why do you think this passage is such an incendiary one for women and men?"

I replied, "Because we are flawed human beings, filled with fear."

I noticed that others to whom that question was posed took more words to explain their answer. And I learned something from each.

But in the end, I liked the simplest answer best.

For the truth of our relationship with God, the world, and our fellow human beings is this: we are motivated by *fear* or *love*.

All our spiritual dilemmas and any inability we have to live up to our beliefs—even our tendency to spiritual pride—can be chalked up to too much fear, not enough love.

The answer is always to increase our capacity to love.

If love is stronger, we'll have more compassion, be more involved in our culture, serve more freely, find more common ground, be better communicators, have more courage to confront problems, and practice more trust in our Creator.

If, on the other hand, we're governed by fear, we'll be withdrawn, self-centered, and uninvolved in the world outside our comfortable little church circle. We'll be like the light hidden under a bowl (Matt. 5:15) rather than those following Jesus who "Let their light so shine before men, that they may see [their] good deeds and praise [their] Father in heaven" (Matt. 5:16).

It's up to us to choose love or to choose fear. God must have known how hard this would be. Again and again in Scripture we're reminded that fear is not from God. Here are just a few:

> "The LORD is my light and my salvation; Whom shall I fear? The LORD is the defense of my life; Whom shall I dread?" (Ps. 27:1, NASB).
>
> "In God I have put my trust, I shall not be afraid. What can man do to me?" (Ps. 56:11, NASB).
>
> "No evil will befall you, Nor will any plague come near your tent. For He will give His angels

charge concerning you, To guard you in all your ways" (Ps. 91:10-11, NASB).

"In righteousness you will be established; You will be far from oppression, for you will not fear; And from terror, for it will not come near you" (Isa. 54:14, NASB).

"Peace I leave with you; My peace I give to you; not as the world gives do I give to you. Do not let your heart be troubled, nor let it be fearful" (John 14:27).

"God has not given us a spirit of timidity, but of power and love and discipline" (2 Tim. 1:7).

"There is no fear in love; but perfect love casts out fear, because fear involves punishment, and the one who fears is not perfected in love" (1 John 4:18).

More than anything, the world needs our love. And we need to understand how important love is in shaping who we are. Our lives can reveal either Jesus or the Pharisee. To reveal Jesus, we need humility and grace.

It's easy to quote the verse reminding us that all have sinned and fall short of the glory of God, but too often the sin of spiritual pride can still make us feel somehow better than, for instance, the lineup of same-sex couples waiting for marriage licenses in San Francisco. It's only by the grace of God and 37 years as a wretched, out-of-control sinner that I know I'm better off only because I have received my Savior.

If Jesus could call out on the Cross, "Father forgive them, for they know not what they do," then surely we can also have compassion for those who don't know Him. We can pray, we can befriend them, and we can live our lives in such a winsome manner that they'll wonder where we got it, that peace that passes all understanding.

Thomas Merton wrote, "Love triumphs, at least in this life, not by eliminating evil once for all but by resisting and overcoming it anew every day."

One thing is certain: it's not political persuasion that will win the hearts or capture the imaginations of those who need God. Only God can do that. But you and I can become the best, most loving followers we can, truly caring for nonbelievers the way God cares for them, and finally to make sure we're not standing in His way.

May God's perfect love cast out our fear,
that we may be better able to carry
whatever message He would have us carry
wherever He would have us carry it.
And oh, may perfect love cast out our fear,
that we may resist and overcome evil anew every day
for the sake of others and to the glory of God,
our Heavenly Father.

NOTES

Chapter 1

Joel Belz, "The Pride Game," *World,* June 28, 2003, 5.

Chapter 2

1. Sheryl Gay Stolberg, "Link Found Between Behavioral Problems and Time in Child Care," *New York Times,* April 19, 2001. Web access at <www.csulb.edu/~kmacd/daycare.htm>.

2. Brian C. Robertson, *There's No Place like Work* (Dallas: Spence Publishing Co., 2000), 24.

3. Ibid.

4. "The Playboy FAQ," <www.playboy.com/worldofplayboy/faq/what.html>.

5. "Resident Population, Selected Characteristics, 1790-2001," Infoplease, <http://www.infoplease.com/ipa/A0772762.html>

6. For one young woman's account of her awakening to the fact that she and her peers had been robbed of a precious and stabilizing commodity, see Wendy Shalit's *A Return to Modesty* (New York: Free Press, January 2000).

7. Barry Maley, "All's Not Fair in No-Fault Divorce," *The Age,* January 6, 2004. Web access at <http://www.theage.com.au/handheld/articles/2004/01/03/1072908951471.html>. Accessed January 8, 2004.

Chapter 3

1. Christina Bellantoni, "Virginia: Birth Control Battle Ensues," *Washington Times,* January 22, 2004, B1.

2. "Bill Aimed at Abortion Education," *Palladium Item* (Richmond, Indiana), January 8, 2004. Web access at <http://www.pal-item.com/news/stories/20040108/localnews/189622.html>. Accessed January 24, 2004.

3. "New Hampshire Court Strikes Down Parental Notification Abortion Law," <http://biz.yahoo.com/prnews/031229/dcm022_1.html>. Accessed January 24, 2004.

4. "Abortion Risks: A List of Major Physical Complications Related to Abortion," fact sheet courtesy of the Elliot Institute, P.O. Box 7348, Springfield, IL 62791. Provides all the medical data and studies for the brief summary of risks stated here. Web access at <http://www.afterabortion.org/physica.html>. Accessed January 24, 2004.

5. Lynn Vincent, "Missing the Link?" *World,* October 18, 2003, 30-31.

6. Coalition on Abortion/Breast Cancer <http://www.abortionbreastcancer.com>.

7. "Doublespeak," Wikipedia, <http://en.wikipedia.org/wiki/doublespeak>. Accessed January 16, 2004.

8. *Medline Plus Medical Dictionary* <http://www2.merriam-webster.com/cgi-bin/mwmednlm?book=Medical&va=partial-birth%20abortion>.

9. Justin Taylor, "Sticker Shock," *World,* January 17, 2004, 43. Although I have not quoted Mr. Taylor directly, I am indebted to his excellent article and flawless logic.

10. *The Revolution* 4(1):4, July 8, 1869, at "Feminist History, Feminists for Life," <http://www.feministsforlife.org/history/foremoth.htm>. Accessed January 21, 2004.

11. Letter to Julia Ward Howe, October 16, 1873, recorded in Howe's diary at Harvard University Library, at "Feminist History, Feminists for Life," <http://www.feministsforlife.org/history/foremoth.htm>. Accessed January 21, 2004.

12. *Woodhull's and Claffin's Weekly* 2(6):4, December 24, 1870, at "Feminist History, Feminists for Life" <http://www.feministsforlife.org/history/foremoth.htm>. Accessed January 21, 2004.

13. "Alice Paul," Wikipedia, <http://en.wikipedia.org/wiki/Alice_Paul>. Accessed August 2, 2005.

14. "Who Has Abortions," *Heartlink,* Focus on the Family's Pregnancy Resource Ministry, <http://www.family.org/pregnancy/general/a0009490.html>. Accessed January 25, 2004.

15. Mission statement, Roe No More, <http://www.roenomore.org/mission/index.htm>. Accessed January 24, 2004.

16. Mary Meehan, "Abortion: The Left Has Betrayed the Sanctity of Life," *Abortion and the American Left,* <http://www.swiss.ai.mit.edu/~rauch/nvp/left.html>. Accessed January 26, 2004.

17. Ibid.

18. Lynn Vincent, "Growing Their Own," *World,* <http://www.worldmag.com/world/issue/01-17-04/cover_2.asp>.

Chapter Four

1. "Have You Heard of the Four Spiritual Laws?" <http://www.greatcom.org/laws/english>.

2. John Cloud, "The Battle over Gay Marriage," *Time*, February 16, 2004.

3. PubMed, National Center for Biotechnology Information, <http://www.ncbi.nlm.nih.gov/entrez/query.fcgi?cmd=Retrieve&db=PubMed&list_uids=9923159&dopt=Abstract>. Accessed February 23, 2004.

4. Andrew Sullivan, "The M-Word: Why It Matters to Me," *Time*, February 10, 2004. Web access at <http://www.andrewsullivan.com/main_article.php?artnum=20040210>. Accessed February 27, 2004.

5. Ibid.

6. Barna Research Group, "Born Again Adults Less Likely to Co-habit, Just as Likely to Divorce," August 6, 2001. <http://www.barna.org/cgi-bin/PagePressRelease.asp?PressReleaseID=95&Reference=C>. Accessed February 27, 2004.

7. "Charles Stanley, Wife Divorce: Atlanta Church Affirms Pastor," *Baptist Press News*, <http://www.baptistpress.org/bpnews.asp?ID=5874>. Accessed February 27, 2004.

8. "Supreme Court Strikes Down Texas Sodomy Law," CNN.com, <http://www.cnn.com/2003/LAW/06/26/scotus.sodomy>. Accessed February 26, 2004.

9. Ibid.

10. Lawrence et al. v. Texas, FindLaw, <http://caselaw.lp.findlaw.com/scripts/getcase.pl?court=US&vol=000&invol=02-102#dissent1>. Accessed February 26, 2004.

11. "Separate Is Seldom . . . Equal" *Boston Globe*, February 4, 2004. Web access at <http://www.boston.com/news/local/massachusetts/articles/2004/02/05/separate_is_seldom_equal>. Accessed February 26, 2004.

12. "Bush Calls for Ban on Same-Sex Marriages," CNN.com, <http://www.cnn.com/2004/ALLPOLITICS/02/24/elec04.prez.bush.marriage>. Accessed February 26, 2004.

13. Star Parker, "Gay Politics, Black Reality" TownHall.com January 12, 2004, <http://www.townhall.com/columnists/GuestColumns/Parker20040112.shtml>. Accessed February 23, 2004.

14. "More Thoughts on Gay Marriage," *World* Magazine Blog, posted by Marvin Olasky February 17, 2004, 11:00 A.M., <http://www.worldmagblog.com/archives/001044.html>.

ABOUT THE AUTHOR . . .

Barbara Curtis was an antiwar activist, radical feminist, and abortion rights activist in Washington, D.C., before moving to San Francisco to experience the more recreational side of the counterculture. Her conversion to Christianity in 1987 changed everything about her. Today she is an award-winning writer whose 700+ publishing credits include articles in *The Washington Times, World,* and *Citizen.* Her books include *Lord, Please Meet Me in the Laundry Room; The Mommy Manual;* and *Dirty Dancing at the Prom and Other Challenges Christian Teens Face.* She is also the mother of 12 children—including three adopted sons with Down syndrome—and grandmother to 10. She and her husband, Tripp—with whom she received the Congressional Angel in Adoption Award—live with their steadily dwindling nest in Waterford, Virginia.

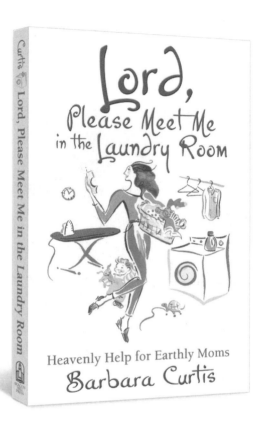

DEDICATION

We dedicate this book to all those who are on their way to becoming survivors. As you do the hard work of getting well, you will soon know the freedom that comes with feeling alive again! It's worth every single difficult and arduous step. We admire you already...

From Megan: To Adam, who continually encourages me to share my story to help others heal. You continue to show me what it means to live freely and humbly, trusting in God all the while. I love our journey! And to Doug Fields, whose endless belief, encouragement, and humility spur me on.

From Jen: To Jay, for being a source of encouragement and strength that allowed me to tell my story in the first place. Without you, I would not be the survivor I am today, and I wouldn't have the courage to help other survivors on the journey. And to R and A, for the work you're doing today to heal and the power your stories will have to help others.

CONTENTS

INTRODUCTION

BECOMING A SECRET SURVIVOR

Secrets. Everyone has them. Some may be as simple as "I lied when I told my best friend I liked her new haircut." Others may be much darker and more painful: "I told everyone I tripped and broke my arm, but actually my dad pushed me down the stairs."

Perhaps you've heard the rhyme little kids say, "Secrets, secrets, are no fun. Secrets, secrets, hurt someone." When we're younger, we don't like it when our friends keep secrets from us because we feel left out. But as we get a little older, the secrets people keep are not so much about others as they are about themselves. Our secrets involve the things we don't like about ourselves, or the things we do that we're ashamed about, or things that have happened to us that we're afraid to let anyone else know about.

No matter what your secret is, there's no doubt it's hurting someone—you. Our secrets carry with them feelings of shame, unworthiness, regret, and fear. As we hold on to our secrets, those feelings eat away at us. Eventually, we begin to believe the lies our secrets are telling us. For instance...

THE GIRL WHO IS BEING PHYSICALLY AND EMOTIONALLY ABUSED BEGINS TO BELIEVE IT WHEN SHE SAYS TO HERSELF, "YOU DESERVE TO BE TREATED THIS WAY. YOU'RE NO GOOD."

THE GIRL WHO IS STARVING HERSELF BELIEVES THE VOICES IN HER HEAD THAT TELL HER, "YOU AREN'T AS THIN/BEAUTIFUL/SMART AS YOU SHOULD BE."

THE GUY WHO IS STRUGGLING WITH PORN ADDICTION THINKS, "THERE MUST BE SOMETHING WRONG WITH YOU IF YOU CAN'T STOP YOURSELF FROM DOING THIS."

THE GIRL WHO WAS RAPED STARTS TO BELIEVE IT'S TRUE WHEN SHE THINKS, "YOU DID SOMETHING TO BRING THAT ON YOURSELF. YOU MUST HAVE ASKED FOR IT."

THE GUY WHO CAN'T STOP USING DRUGS AND ALCOHOL BEGINS TO BELIEVE HIS OWN LIES: "GOD DOESN'T LOVE YOU. HOW COULD HE AFTER ALL YOU'VE DONE?"

Whatever secrets you are carrying, you are not alone. Maybe you don't know anyone else who feels the way you feel, or who is struggling with the problem you have. That's probably because other people who are dealing with those issues have hidden them away as their own dark secrets, too. Our culture is a place where performing, pleasing, and perfection are of the highest value. They are touted in movies, on TV, in ads. As a result, people appear perfect; they act like everything is fine. It makes us think *we* have to be all put together, too. We think that if anyone ever knew about our deepest secrets, then we'd be hated, mocked, talked about, and humiliated. So we think it's easier and safer to just keep our secrets to ourselves and try to survive them.

But the reality is that our secrets eat away at us. Secrets break us down emotionally, physically, spiritually, and relationally. The only way to really survive is to break the power our secrets have over us—by telling someone else.

Survivors. You've seen the TV show, or you've heard stories of people who managed to escape death when their plane crashed or they were trapped in an avalanche. They're called *survivors*. But you don't have to go to a deserted island or have a near-death experience to be a survivor.

Those of us who are brave enough to share our secrets are also survivors. When we tell someone else about the pain we've been hiding, we break free of the power that secret had over us. We begin to heal. And we realize there is strength to be found when we share our secrets. Many people discover that when they finally take the courageous step of sharing secrets they've kept hidden, they experience new life and hope for who they are, and who they can be.

Like most of those survivors you hear about in the news, these secret survivors want to tell others about their experiences. They want to make sure others know so they don't have to be trapped by their personal secrets. They want others to find healing, to break the power of the secret, and to escape the pain and shame that holds them captive.

As you read *Secret Survivors*, you'll encounter eight true stories of people like you—people who once had a secret; people who carried a great deal of pain from what they held inside. Each of those people found a way to share that secret with someone and begin the journey toward healing. While all the stories are true, the names have been changed to protect the innocent (and the guilty).

We (Jen and Megan) have included our own stories in these pages because we, too, are Secret Survivors!

We know personally the destructive power secrets can hold over us. We know how secrets can kill the very lives we are intended to live. But we also know the freedom you find when you reveal your secret. Surviving a secret will make you feel empowered, alive, and courageous. It will make you believe in yourself again. Like the other people profiled in this book, we've found that sharing our secrets with a trusted, caring confidant was the beginning of the journey toward surviving.

Of course, the healing doesn't happen overnight. For most people, the struggle doesn't end the minute we find the courage to speak out. Healing takes time. We've also found there are some who share their secret with someone, or even with lots of people, but still never move to any deeper level of hope and healing, because they just weren't truly ready to walk the hard road to healing. But in most cases, sharing one's story can play a dynamic and life-changing role if the secret carrier is ready and willing. One thing is certain: Staying silent is never the answer.

It is our hope that as you meet each of these courageous survivors, perhaps their stories will connect with your own pain, your struggle to understand God in the midst of your hurt, and your desire to be whole again. In the end, we hope these stories will inspire you to become a survivor—to reach out to someone you trust and share your secret.

Everyone has secrets, but not everyone survives the heavy burden those secrets can place on them. It's time to stop letting your secret have power over you.

It's time for you to tell someone your story and become a survivor.

We've created a place for you to start. At the end of this book we've offered you some ideas on how you can tell your own story. Sometimes it's easier to write your story out—even changing your name if it's easier for you to think of it as someone else. You'll also find additional resources for help with the issues found in this book.

We want to help you share your secret so you can become a survivor! If you're not sure who you can trust with your secret, you can visit SecretSurvivors.com, where you'll find a place you can tell your story anonymously. We will be there to pray for you and to point you toward more resources that can help in your healing journey.

Wherever you go to tell your story, know that opening up about your secret is the first step on your road to wholeness. We have traveled a similar "secret" road, and we believe there are people who love you and are willing to walk beside you. So here's to your journey toward becoming a Secret Survivor. May God fill you with strength, courage, and hope as you heal.

You are not alone.

Jen and Megan

CHAPTER ONE

KAT
A SURVIVOR OF DATE RAPE

Kat is a strong woman with a lively personality that draws others to her. But beyond her energetic spirit, there is a compassionate woman who understands pain, shame, and healing. She's committed to helping others who are in pain because of the journey she's made herself—a journey through hurt to a place of healing that enables her to shine and bring joy to everyone around her. So here's the story of Kat—a survivor of date rape.

It was a warm evening in October. They were at his grandparents' house, alone in the backyard. They looked up at the full moon as Dave began touching her with tender kisses and gentle strokes of her hair. And as he kissed her, he would say, "I love you...I love you." Kat felt so loved inside.

But in an instant Dave's tender gentleness turned into a more aggressive touch. His sweet voice grew harsh. He forced her onto the ground, as she cried, "No...No." She struggled, confused by what was happening. But she could not stop him. He forced himself inside of her and, within seconds, it was over. It all happened so quickly, but Kat recalls every vivid detail. Her boyfriend had sex with her against her will.

She lay on the ground as Dave quickly got up, adjusted himself, and looked at her tear-stained face. "What the hell is the matter with you?" he asked harshly. "I love you. Get up."

Disillusioned, she thought to herself, "He's right. What is the matter with *me*?" So she picked herself up, dusted herself off, and acted like it never happened.

Nearly five years later, Kat sat in her college chapel service listening to another woman share her own story of being date raped. Kat's stomach was in knots as she listened. "I felt as though the speaker was telling *my* story. That was the first time I realized that what had happened to me when I was only 14 was not my fault. I had been date raped."

Born just a few days after the fourth of July, Kat always lived up to the nickname her mother gave her—"firecracker baby." As the youngest of four girls, it didn't take Kat long to figure out she loved people and any attention she could get from them. She discovered a talent for roller-skating, so she would invite all the neighbors to pay a dime to attend her "shows." As she rolled into aerials and cartwheels, the "audience" cheered! From that point on, Kat worked hard to gain the applause and praise of those around her.

Kat also loved to play. She and her youngest sister, Allison, spent many hours up in the old wooden tree house their dad had built—playing, singing, dancing, and laughing. They also went on lots of family trips in their motor home. They went all over the country—usually with their boat or motorcycle in tow. Looking back, these are among Kat's fondest memories.

Her family never missed church on Sunday. Mom would make sure everyone was dressed like perfect little ladies, and then dad would pile all the girls—Karen, Ann, Allison, and Kat—into the family station wagon. "I hated church, mostly because it was boring, but also because my school was part of the church—it was like I could never escape."

But church is the place Kat learned to be on her very best behavior. When the girls misbehaved, they were spanked. However, when they behaved well, they were rewarded with a piece of candy from the local 7-Eleven store. The girls loved candy, so they were usually on their best behavior.

When Kat was nine, the family went to New York City and saw the Broadway musical, "Little Orphan Annie." It inspired Kat like nothing else, and it became her goal to sound just like Annie. Day after day, she and Allison would sing "Tomorrow" at the top of their lungs, hoping someone would hear and compliment their talent.

Kat soon found herself singing all the time. She took private voice lessons for 10 years, and began singing professionally during that time. Whenever her parents had guests over, Kat was the entertainment. She performed everywhere she could—musicals, churches, and even her tree house (so all the neighbors could hear!). When people clapped and cheered, she felt like she was special—like she was loved and valued and worth something. It was during these experiences that Kat started to determine how loved she was by how well she performed—in every area of her life.

KAT STARTED TO DETERMINE HOW LOVED SHE WAS BY HOW WELL SHE PERFORMED—IN EVERY AREA OF HER LIFE.

Like many other girls, Kat went through junior high concerned about her body and obsessed with boys. Shortly after her 14th birthday, she started attending a new youth group in a local church. That's when she first locked eyes with Dave. That night he offered to drive her home and she accepted.

Dave was almost 17, and Kat was flattered by his attention. When they got to her house, he asked her out to the movies and she accepted immediately. The only problem was her parents' rule—the girls couldn't date until they turned 16. But Kat was so thrilled to have the attention of a boy she liked that she decided to lie to her parents. "The entire youth group is going to the drive-in movie this Friday," she told them with convincing excitement. "Can I go?" Her parents said yes—up until this point, she'd never given them any reason not to trust her.

From that first date, they were hooked. They soon started seeing each other nearly every day, and Kat's parents were thrilled she was spending so much time with the "youth group." As the weeks went by, Kat began to feel things for Dave she'd never felt before; she trusted him and cared deeply for him.

About a month after they started dating, Kat and Dave went to a friend's house one night to hang out in the hot tub, since the friend's parents were out of town. They joked around and laughed, and Dave gently kissed Kat and told her how much he loved being near her. Then he started to touch her breasts, and she began to cry. She'd never been touched like that before, and she was not comfortable with it. But Dave's response put her at ease. "I'm sorry, I love you. Let's pray." She believed him, especially since he told her he loved her. So far in life, Kat's experiences had taught her that people who love you don't intentionally hurt you.

But the next night they went back to the hot tub and he started again. Except this time he tried to go even further. Again, Kat cried, and Dave was quick to respond, "I'm sorry, I love you. Let's pray." Kat believed him again. In her mind he was her first love, and she believed he loved her and he loved God.

The next time Dave touched her, he proved he was not worthy of her trust. This was the night he violated her terribly, by having sex with her against her will. It was a night she would never, ever forget.

She walked away from that experience a different girl. She thought it was her fault. In a matter of seconds her world was turned upside-down and nothing would ever be the same—not her family, her friends, her school, God, and especially the way she viewed herself. And in the days and months that followed, she felt surrounded by a thick, dark fog. She felt the beating of a constant pain inside her.

Two weeks after the night when Dave forced her to have sex, Kat was getting ready to sing a solo at church when Dave walked in. He came over to her and said, "I never loved you. It's over," and walked away.

She stood there in disbelief. She wondered, "How could he do that? How could he give himself to me and then dump me like nothing ever happened? As if *sex* never happened!" She wanted to scream at him, but she couldn't find any words. She loved him and hated him at the same time—and it left her confused and devastated. She fell deeper into the fog and contemplated suicide.

She wrote a suicide letter to her family and then tore it into pieces. Deep inside she knew that wasn't the answer.

But Kat didn't know how to handle all the pain she was feeling. She started doing things she'd never done before—ditching school, sneaking out in the middle of the night, drinking, experimenting with drugs, and hooking up with random guys. Her pain hit an all-time low when she woke up in a motel room one morning next to a guy she barely knew. She had to ask him what they'd done together, because she'd been too drunk to remember. She was in a downward spiral and life felt out of control. Her dreams were broken and her heart was broken.

"It was like I was trying to drown out my pain with anything that might distract me," Kat recalls. "But I couldn't escape the pain, and people started to notice." It wasn't long before her parents, who loved her deeply, were catching her in her own lies. She was grounded for days, weeks, and even months on end. But it didn't make her change. In fact, it made her rebel even more.

As an innocent nine-year-old, Kat had dreamed of being Annie. As an infatuated 14-year-old, she'd lost her virginity against her will. And now, suddenly, she was 18—a legal adult—and her life was spinning out of control.

But the date rape was still her secret. No one knew what had happened with Dave. Kat tried to cover her pain and brokenness by performing even more, trying to appear like she had it all together. She sang her heart out to get applause and dated every willing guy—anything to make her feel accepted and loved.

When she was 19, Kat started attending a Christian college, on a vocal music scholarship. As a freshman she often wore skimpy clothing to get attention from guys. She remembers very vividly a day when another girl gently confronted her about the way she dressed. It shocked Kat. She didn't know her efforts to gain attention and approval were so obvious. "Slowly I began to realize that the feeling I got when a guy gave me a look or a smile didn't really satisfy my deep longing for love and acceptance."

Kat experienced a lot of changes when she started college. But during her first semester, something unexplainable happened. Overnight, she lost her singing voice. Doctors couldn't explain the loss. She saw the top vocal specialist in Los Angeles, and his words shocked her. "Kat, you will never sing again."

She listened in disbelief. "What do you mean I'll never be able to sing again?" she asked. "There's got to be *something* you can do. I'm a singer! That's what I'm supposed to do with my life!" But there was nothing any doctor could do. For years Kat had dreamed she'd make it as a singer. She'd been told she was good enough to make it in New York. And now, in a single moment, she'd lost her scholarship, her dream, and the focus of her life. Kat cried and asked herself a million questions: "What will I do now? Who am I without my singing voice? Why would God allow this to happen to me?" It wasn't until years later that she would find answers to her questions.

It was just a week after hearing that news from her doctor that Kat found herself sitting in the college chapel, listening to a woman who shared her own story of being date raped. Kat sat, with her stomach in knots, as the woman spoke of how her experience had led her to look for love and acceptance from men to ease her pain. She said it had taken years for her to realize and accept how deeply God loved her.

"As I listened, I felt like she was telling *my* story. For the very first time, I realized that what had happened to me when I was just 14 wasn't my fault." The words rang through her ears: *It was not my fault. It was not my fault.* Kat ran to her dorm room, grabbed her teddy bear, and curled into a ball. She cried until she had no tears left, and then she called her mom. Kat could barely speak the words of her long-locked secret: "Mom...I...was...date...raped." It was the first time she had told anyone.

Her mom comforted her over the phone. She reminded Kat of how much she and her dad loved her, and said they'd do whatever it took to get her the help she needed. "You're going to be okay, honey. It's going to be all right." Kat felt a strange sense of peace for the first time in a long time.

The very next day Kat began meeting with a counselor. And week by week, month by month, and year by year, her life began to change. She learned a lot in those years. She learned that keeping that secret—what had happened to her at age 14—was only hurting her. She learned to trust herself. She learned to have faith in God again. Eventually, she learned she could actually forgive Dave. And she learned that her true identity was not as a singer, a girlfriend, a student, or a successful career woman. Her identity was as the woman that God created her to be—with gifts, talents, and abilities that she could use to make a difference in the world.

TODAY, KAT KNOWS SHE IS LOVED AND ACCEPTED JUST AS SHE IS

Kat is quick to point out that she didn't learn any of those things overnight. She spent years believing she was unlovable (unless a guy was attracted to her) and unworthy (unless she was offering something to someone else) and unacceptable (unless she was performing). It took years for Kat to replace those lies with the truth. She had to remind herself daily who she really was, and that she was deeply loved.

During her junior year of college, Kat clung to a few verses in the Bible that she prayed for herself everyday. She'd get on her knees and tell herself:

Kat, you were bought with a price. (1 Corinthians 6:20)

Kat, you are a new creation. (2 Corinthians 5:17)

Kat, you are chosen by God, holy and dearly loved. (Colossians 3:12)

Kat, be strong and courageous. Do not be afraid; do not be discouraged, for the Lord your God will be with you wherever you go. (Joshua 1:9)

As she repeated these promises from God each day and learned to trust her own voice, the truth began to sink in. Today, Kat knows she is loved and accepted just as she is—even if she can't sing, and even if she's not the center of attention.

When Kat looks back on her journey, she sees that God never wastes a pain. She believes that God can take even our most tumultuous and tragic experiences and use them to help us—and others—grow emotionally, spiritually, and mentally. But she knows from experience that, in order for any good to come from our pain, we have to do our part. We have to choose how we handle our pain, or else our pain will handle us.

Kat buried her pain for years, and it had repercussions in every area of her life. But once she was able to face the reality of being a date rape victim, and once she dealt with the painful effects it had on her life, she found a way to reach out to other victims, to gently guide them through their own pain. And as she's been able to use her own experience to help others, she's come to realize her pain was not wasted.

Today, Kat shares her story without hesitation, in an effort to help break down the walls of secrets we all carry in our lives. She serves as a pastor to hurting students at her local church and everyday helps students get open about their hidden pain. Her biggest support is from her husband, whom she's been married to for more than 10 years. Together, they know the truth that there is a way out of the secrets that control us, and that there is always help for our hurt.

REFLECTIONS

Take a minute to reflect on Kat's story. Close your eyes and imagine what it must have felt like to be a 14-year-old girl who was brutally betrayed by someone she thought loved her. Maybe you've felt that kind of betrayal yourself.

1. Have you ever felt like Kat—used, abused, and discarded like a piece of trash? When? What happened? Who was there? How did you feel? What did you do after that?

2. Do you ever feel like you have to perform to be accepted? Whose acceptance are you seeking? What do feel like you have to do to be acceptable to them?

3. What do you think would happen if you stopped performing in order to get noticed or gain people's acceptance?

4. Use the assurances from Scripture that are printed below to help you remember who you really are, and what your value truly is. Write your name in each blank, and remember to tell yourself these things every day.

____________________________, you were bought with a price. (1 Corinthians 6:20)

____________________________, you are a new creation. (2 Corinthians 5:17)

____________________________, you are chosen by God, holy and dearly loved. (Colossians 3:12)

____________________________, be strong and courageous. Do not be afraid; do not be discouraged, for the Lord your God will be with you wherever you go. (Joshua 1:9)

CHAPTER TWO

DARIA
A SURVIVOR OF CUTTING

Under her gentle and quiet demeanor, Daria is a combination of brilliance and grace, wisdom and depth. But not all that long ago, she was a dead girl walking. Dressed in all black, with thick make-up and noticeable scars, there was a heaviness that seemed to surround her. Today, all that has changed. Daria is a joy to be around, with a passion for life that's contagious. Now you get to share in the story of her miraculous transformation...

If you'd seen Daria as a child, you might not have noticed her. She was the shy, chubby girl, sitting quietly in the back of the room. She went home after school and read books or wrote her thoughts down. Even though she had a few friends, she rarely hung around after school or went out with friends. She was a loner.

Daria lived with her mom and grandma—who couldn't stand each other. Her home was not a quiet or happy place. The walls rang with fighting and screaming most of the time. It was not unusual for her mom and grandma to drag Daria into it, and she quickly learned to hold her own in the arguments.

Her dad left before she was even born. She's never met him, but her mom used to tell stories of him being a liar and a schizophrenic. She grew up wondering what it would be like to have a dad, especially when she saw other kids with their dads. She tried not to care, but deep inside she couldn't help but wonder. "I felt like I was worthless, since my own father wouldn't try to be a part of my life." But since her mom and grandma hated him so much, Daria had no choice but to hide her feelings from them—which made her feel even more alone.

Daria was a smart and creative kid. She knew from a young age that she wanted to be a writer, although she did have a fleeting desire to be a firefighter. She dreamed of going to Stanford University, since people in her family had gone there. She worked really hard to keep her grades up, so she wouldn't upset her mom or grandma.

The expectations Daria's mom and grandma placed on her were beyond what most kids her age could handle.

When she was about seven, her mom took her to Jenny Craig because she thought Daria was too fat. It was scary and embarrassing. She'd step on the scale, and the adults would talk as if she weren't even there, "Yeah, she needs to lose weight. She should go to meetings." Daria sat in meetings with her mom; she was the only kid there in a room full of adults. "Most of the time I'd just stare off and daydream," she recalls, "trying to deny the fact that I was actually there."

One of the few upsides to her experience with weight loss as a kid was joining karate. She was black belt before she started fourth grade. She competed in tournaments in states around hers, and even traveled to Hawaii with her mom for one competition. Those tournaments are among the few happy memories she has from her childhood.

Anger and hatred were the only emotions that were acceptable to express in Daria's childhood home. So when Daria was sad or scared—or even happy—she didn't feel free to show those feelings. Even love was rarely expressed in their house. She felt loved at times, but the words "I love you" were never spoken. In fact, Daria remembers sitting in the car when she was about 10 and asking, "Why don't you say 'I love you' to each other?" Her mom and grandma just looked at each other, so she decided to drop the conversation. "I knew they loved me," Daria remembers, "but I only believed that because they'd buy me things—not because they told me so."

Daria learned that her emotions had to remain her own. In order to deal with how she felt, at a very young age she began to hit her head against the wall whenever she was upset. "For whatever reason, the pain made me feel better." She realized she could exchange her mental and emotional pain for physical pain; at least that's what she thought she was accomplishing.

After a while, Daria found that hitting her head against the wall just didn't do enough for her. She had to express her pain differently and take it to the next level so she would feel better. One day when she was in second grade she got a C on a test. She was so afraid to take it home and show her mom. Almost instinctively, Daria reached into her desk and took out a ruler with a metal edge. She asked to be excused to the bathroom, and when she was alone there she scratched her forearm and drew a tiny drop of blood. She felt immediate release. Later that day, her teacher saw the cut and asked what had happened. Daria lied and said she fell on the playground, and her teacher was fine with that answer. "I didn't want to have to answer any more questions about my cuts, so I decided that hitting my head against the wall was a better option—because it didn't leave marks people would notice."

Whether she was cutting or banging her head, Daria felt better when she did it. It helped her catch her breath so she could move on. But as her emotional pain increased, so did her need for more physical pain.

In sixth grade the cutting got much worse. She began using knives and razor blades, and she started cutting deeper. She was so desperate at times that she even snuck out of youth group to cut herself in the church bathroom. Cutting quickly became an addiction for her. Without doing it, she just couldn't deal. The sight of her blood allowed her to feel; it was like breathing to her. It was as if it cleared her head so she could grasp everything that was going on. In a strange way, the pain and the blood were soothing to her.

DARIA CUT NOT BECAUSE SHE WANTED TO DIE—SHE CUT BECAUSE SHE WANTED TO SURVIVE.

At one point during middle school, Daria tried to stop cutting. Her youth pastor noticed the cuts and confronted her. She felt like he laid a guilt trip on her, so she agreed to stop. But all cutters know you just don't *stop* without finding another way to deal. Her pain ran so deep that she quickly found another way to cope. She stopped eating. In the sixth grade she went from 180 pounds to 110 pounds in six months. But it was only when other people pointed out her weight loss that she realized she'd swapped one problem for another. Still, it felt good to be in control of her body. And when things were really bad at home, she would bang her head, cut her body, and not eat—all at the same time.

Her youth pastor was the only person who'd ever talked to Daria about her cutting. But when it seemed to be growing worse, he told her mom. "That was a very bad day," Daria remembers. "My mom yelled and cried to the youth pastor about not being a good enough mom. It felt like she turned all the attention off of me and my problem, and made it all about her." Daria was used to her mom doing that. Fortunately, her mom did want Daria to get help. She loved Daria as best she could.

Initially, her mom considered sending Daria to a residential treatment facility. Daria was thrilled about the possibility of getting out of the house and away from the chaos of her everyday life. But eventually Daria's mom and grandma decided Daria needed to learn to cope with her problems in the midst of her crazy house and family, rather than being sent away and then coming back into the craziness. So instead she was sent to a therapist.

Daria went through phases when she wanted to get help, and other times when she didn't. So when the therapist visits ended, she wasn't all that upset. And her mom was pleased she didn't have to pay for Daria's therapy any longer.

Eventually, Daria started to get really tired of the life she was living. She used to feel unnoticed—now it seemed like she was attracting too much attention. If the people at school weren't talking about her cutting, they were talking about her family or her goth style. She felt like her life was a three-ring circus. Sure, some people would even offer support to her, but she didn't really feel like they were genuine.

Eventually, she overdosed. "I wasn't trying to kill myself," she says. "I just wanted to escape for a little while—to sleep my days away." That day, after she took too many pills, she called her youth pastor. He called her mom, and they all went to the hospital. She spent 72 hours in the psych ward of the hospital. After that she decided to make a change.

At church one day, Daria saw a flyer for a teen support group called Life Hurts, God Heals. She and a friend decided to check it out—and they were shocked by what they experienced. The minute she heard the testimony of the leader of the group, Daria and her friend realized this was something that was meant for them. Eventually, Daria opened up to other people in the group and began talking about her own pain for the first time in her life.

"I'd never been *that* open before; it was too scary. But in this group, something was different. I felt safe." Daria was able to embrace the fact that people actually cared about her and that she was worth something. She decided it was time to move on and get out of the destructive patterns that were dominating her life. Through the eight steps in Life Hurts, God Heals, and with the support and encouragement of the other people in the group, Daria was able to start her own healing journey and stop cutting.

Like most other people who cut, Daria cut not because she wanted to die—she cut because she wanted to survive. "I felt like I was just trying to make it through everyday life, but I couldn't express what I was feeling besides showing it on my arms."

In the beginning, Daria didn't hide her cuts, but as it got worse, she worked very hard to keep her secret pain hidden. Now she talks openly about why she cut, what it did for her, and how she was able to heal from the pain that drove her to cut. Daria spent years struggling alone, but she encourages other people who are hurting themselves to get help. She discovered there actually are people out there who want to help, people who actually care.

SHE DISCOVERED THERE ACTUALLY ARE PEOPLE OUT THERE WHO WANT TO HELP, PEOPLE WHO ACTUALLY CARE.

When she was in the depths of her pain, Daria wishes she'd felt more love and care from the people around her. As she moved through the stages of recovery, hugs became vital to her— even though she'd always shied away from expressing affection. Those hugs were a reminder that people cared. And having someone who was verbally supportive made all the difference for Daria. "It helped make up for all the horrible stuff I'd heard from my mom all my life, and it reinforced the good things I was doing."

Today, Daria has big dreams of writing a book and changing the world. When she struggles with life these days (and she does because she still lives at home), she writes and she relies more heavily on God. When she's having a bad day, she'll open her Bible or the old diary where she journaled throughout her healing process, and she'll be reminded she's strong enough to get through whatever her current problem is. She no longer hides her pain or her scars. "When people ask about my scars, I tell my story. I hope that the story I've lived will help save someone else, that it'll encourage anyone who is cutting to tell someone else, and to get the help they need to heal."

REFLECTIONS

Everyone hurts, and we all deal with our hurts differently. Maybe you stuff your pain back inside, or maybe you punch a pillow. Maybe you self-medicate, or maybe you inflict pain on yourself.

1. How do you deal with your own emotional pain?

2. Have you ever felt like Daria—that hurting yourself makes you feel more alive? If so, what other things have you experienced in life that make you feel alive, and how can you find more healthy and life-giving ways of dealing with your struggles?

3. If you're hiding your pain from the people around you, to whom can you turn for help?

4. Do you believe that God is capable of healing your deepest wounds? Spend a few minutes talking to God and ask for healing in your life.

If you or someone you care for is dealing with pain in a way that can only bring more pain, there is hope. Here are some practical ways you can help:

What if you're struggling with self-injurious behaviors?

- Tell someone. Find someone you can trust, even if it's the authors of this book. Let a trusted friend into your pain and let that person help you begin to heal. Sharing your secret is the first step in healing.
- Look in the back of this book for resources and Web sites where you can learn how to cope with the struggles of life, and where you can find support to help you stop hurting yourself.
- Ask God and the people around you to pour love into you. Ask them to help you feel so full of love that you don't want to let a drop of it leave you.

What if someone you love is self-injuring?

- Talk to that person. Ask what's going on, but do so in a caring way, without judgment. Get a trusted adult into the situation—a youth pastor, a teacher, a parent—who can help your friend find help.

- Love your friend—no matter what. Let that person know you care and that you want to help. And remember, you can't fix that person, no matter how much you might want to. Your friend needs to decide to get help; but you can offer support along the way and love that person through it all.
- Look in the back of this book for resources and Web sites that can help you understand more about what your friend is struggling with, and where you can point that person when he or she is ready to get help.

CHAPTER THREE

WHITNEY
A SURVIVOR OF ABORTION

Whitney is a beautiful woman with talent, charm, and a sweet demeanor. She's a fabulous mother who spends her days caring for her two wonderful children. As is the case with most survivors, you'd never know her painful story if you didn't ask and she didn't tell. Whitney is a reminder that there is a story behind every face...and her story will encourage you. Meet Whitney.

"I can vividly remember walking into the clinic. All the patients had little slippers on their feet, and all the chairs were lined up on each side of the room, feeling like a cold and sterile barbershop." Whitney took her place alongside the other young girls and women.

Each girl sat in her gown waiting for her turn. Whitney noticed that a 16-year-old girl next to her was with her mom. "I couldn't fathom the idea that my mom would ever bring me here, but I wished my mom were with me." Finally, it was her turn.

Whitney's stomach was in knots as the doctor did the procedure. It took only a few minutes; but the memory has lasted for years. She lay on the table with her feet in the stirrups as the doctor used a vacuum to take the life from within her. The sound was horrific. It would haunt her and give her nightmares for years.

When it was over, she drove herself back to college and laid on her dorm room bed for days, curled up in a ball. No one back home would ever have suspected she'd be having an abortion. Not Whitney—she was the straight-A student, the student body president of her high school, the girl from the homecoming court. This wasn't supposed to be happening to her a few months into her first year of college. Not even her roommate knew what had happened. "I was miserable, and my life became unbearable."

Whitney was the first born, and she was the typical overachiever: outgoing and extraverted. She loved being good, but even more, she loved it when people noticed her for being good. "I spent a lot of my childhood following the rules, getting good grades, and being a happy, good girl," she recalls.

From most angles Whitney's childhood was pretty ideal. Her family was stable, her parents loved each other, and even her little brother, Jake, didn't get on her nerves too much. On Saturday mornings she and Jake would watch cartoons and eat cereal until it was time to get up and go outside. They spent many days playing from morning till night (or at least from after school until dinner) in the cul-de-sac where they lived, which was filled with all the neighborhood kids. During the summers, her whole family would head out to Arkansas to visit Meemaw and Granddad. Some of her favorite memories were of the whole family playing board games, or waterskiing on the lake near her grandparents' home.

Whitney loved the fact that her entire family was always very close. But it was her mom who was Whitney's closest friend. After school she'd sit at the kitchen table and tell her mom everything from her day. "I knew I could always talk to my mom and that she would listen." She couldn't imagine ever keeping a secret from her mom because her mom was always such a caring listener.

Her dad had grown up without parents. His grandparents raised him, and Whitney thought he was a great father, especially since his own dad hadn't been there for him. Her dad was a man who'd made something of himself, by himself. He'd put himself through school and even got a Ph.D., so he had high expectations for Whitney to be successful.

Throughout her childhood Whitney's parents made her go to church. She didn't mind this because all her friends were there and they did fun things. But the older she got, the more she felt like church was mostly a lot of rules. She remembers when her entire sixth-grade Sunday school class had to memorize the book of James, which is all about doing "works." It seemed her whole world was about looking, doing, and performing well so others would approve of her. Even at church. And as a result, when she was 18, Whitney decided she didn't want to go to church anymore. "My dad cried when I told them this," she remembers. "It was the first time I'd ever seen him cry."

While Whitney felt very loved by her parents, her boyfriends were also a very significant part of her life as a teenager. She didn't date around; she had very serious, long-term relationships with guys. When she was 16 she started dating Mike, who was 18, even though her parents forbid her to. It was the first time she remembers lying to her mom and dad, but she and Mike snuck around all the time. He was a needy guy, but also kind of a jerk. He wouldn't show up when he said he would, and he was considered a "bad boy." Being the good girl she was, Whitney thought she could change him—but it just didn't work out between them.

The sneaking around with Mike set Whitney up for her next relationship. Keith was a surfer, totally laid back, and really nice. She met Keith after she changed schools and began attending a very small Christian school, and they dated during their junior and senior years of high school. They dated for a while before they had sex for the first time. "I felt like I wanted to experience the 'whole love' completion of our relationship, and that's what sex meant to me."

SHE'S NOT SURE HOW OR WHEN THEY DECIDED, BUT SHE AND KEITH DECIDED SHE'D HAVE AN ABORTION.

Keith and Whitney kept the sex a secret from everyone. Not even their best friends knew they were having sex. Whitney felt like this was the person she'd be with forever, which is one reason it was so easy to fall into the cycle they began. They'd have sex, and because they'd grown up in the church, they would then feel guilty. They'd talk about it and decide not to go that far again—but then they'd do it anyway. Soon Whitney found she had no self-control. "I don't even think I was afraid of being caught," she remembers, yet she kept it a secret from everyone, including her very best friend—her mom. Whitney couldn't bring herself to tell her mom. Her mom saw Whitney as her pure, sweet daughter. This would completely tarnish how her mom saw her. So Whitney kept it all inside.

Two years into the relationship, she and Keith were preparing to graduate from high school. Whitney had to make the tough decision about where to go to college. She'd been raised to be her own person and make her own decisions, but she really loved Keith. It took her three agonizing months—but in the end she made the difficult decision of going to school in another state, hours away from him.

That fall Whitney decided to come home from college on the weekend of her high school's homecoming. She'd been feeling really sick, so she went to the family doctor while she was home. "It never dawned on me that I could be pregnant, so when the doctor told me I was, I was stunned." Whitney had no idea how to deal with the news. Immediately, she thought about the acne medication she'd been taking. It said on the packaging that you shouldn't take it while pregnant because it could cause serious birth defects. Suddenly she had horrible thoughts running through her mind. She went home from the doctor and called Keith. He came down from school, which was only a few hours away, and they talked. They didn't know what to do. She's not sure how or when they decided, but she and Keith decided she'd have an abortion.

In her mind, Whitney explained it away because of her medication. She told herself it was an act of mercy—that the child would likely have been born deformed and would have had to suffer through life. Once she was back at school, Keith wired her the money (which he'd borrowed from a friend), and Whitney took the hour-long drive to the clinic by herself. It was a drive she would always remember.

After the abortion, things got so bad for Whitney that she decided to transfer schools midsemester, hoping another school would give her a fresh start and help make things better. But by February she was so lonely that Keith decided to come out to see her. Whitney was feeling so empty and in need of love, which she still equated with sex. So they had sex—which made her feel loved for the moment.

That weekend, Whitney got pregnant again. "I still don't know how someone can make the same wretched mistake twice, but I was in such a downward spiral that I just kept going until I hit bottom." Apparently she hadn't gotten there yet.

She called Keith after she found out she was pregnant, and again he wired her money. This time she had a friend at school she trusted enough to talk about it with. Her friend went with her to a "parenthood clinic" where the people there were supposed to help her consider her options. Sadly, the option of abortion was presented as if it were a simple procedure without any physical or emotional consequences. "No one ever discussed with me that I was likely to experience feelings of deep remorse, guilt, depression, and despair, possibly for the rest of my life. No one ever encouraged me to call my parents and share with them the truth of my situation. At age 18 I was legally old enough to make this decision for myself, but inside I was longing for someone to nudge me toward opening up to my parents for real help." But instead she returned to the same sterile place and had another abortion.

After that, Whitney lost herself completely. The first abortion changed her quite a bit; the second one altered her in every way. She became an empty shell, and eventually transferred to Keith's school. Shortly after she arrived there, Keith confessed he'd cheated on her. She was devastated. She'd never felt more alone. The one person who knew her deepest, darkest secrets could no longer be trusted.

The pain didn't stop there. Keith's sister, who had become a good friend of Whitney's, had gotten pregnant and decided to have the baby and give it up for adoption. Whitney was in the room with her before the labor began, and being in a place where so many babies are born, feeling the guilt she was carrying, she crumbled. But on the outside, she kept pretending like everything was okay. She was still carrying her pain on her own.

Whitney tried to make everything okay in her life. She became a resident assistant in her dorm, ended her relationship with Keith for good, and started going back to church. She even started dating Alex, a guy who lived in her dorm. But she could only hold it together for a couple of weeks at a time—then she'd crash. She was skipping classes and flunking out. "I was no longer the straight-A student I'd always been. And the guilt I was carrying—especially for lying to my parents—was eating me up."

Alex was the one positive in her life at the time. Whitney felt safe with him, and eventually decided to share her secret. She was so afraid he'd think differently of her or leave her when he found out what she'd done. But he was so loving and kind to her in spite of her secret. They dated for the next fours years, off and on, but Whitney was never really okay. She'd often end up crying so hard she was gasping for air. Alex told her she needed to talk to her mom about it. He assured her she'd get through it—even though it would be hard.

Telling her mom about the abortions was one of the hardest conversations of Whitney's life. Her mom was broken, but not because of disappointment or anger as Whitney had expected. "My mom was broken because I had been alone through it all." Whitney didn't know what to think of her mom's response. She couldn't comprehend it. Her mom wasn't mad? Whitney was shocked. In fact, her mom extended her grace despite what she'd done. She realized her mom loved and accepted her, even if she wasn't perfect.

Whitney made her mom promise she would keep the secret from her dad. Her mom agreed, but sent Whitney to therapy all summer.

Whitney's healing process began on the day she shared her secret with her mom. But she still had to spend a long time in counseling, dealing with issues surrounding her guilt and shame. "It took me years to erase the sound of the vacuum that took my babies, and years to forgive myself for choosing to abort them, but eventually I did."

Whitney also found the courage to tell her dad about the abortions. He broke down and sobbed. He couldn't believe his baby girl had been through all that alone. His forgiveness astounded Whitney. "It was less painful to tell my parents than I thought it would be." She always knew she had a gift in her parents before, but now she *really* knew.

As Whitney continued to heal, she and Alex decided to get married. They have since had two wonderful children together. "I live with the guilt and shame of what I did; I think about those two unborn children every day." Whitney discovered that her choices caused her so much more pain because she went through it alone. If she had told the two people in her life who loved her most and could have helped her, it might have saved her years of pain. She continues to heal and has reconnected with God in new ways. The road to healing is a long one. But when you're not alone on the journey, it's a lot easier to carry on.

REFLECTIONS

Whitney says, "One of the hardest things about healing from an abortion is that, in other situations—like if you were raped or molested—part of the healing is realizing that what happened was not your fault. There comes a time when you are released somewhat because you realize it wasn't your fault. There is no such release from that with an abortion. You're responsible for your decision, and you have to live with that...For a long time it was hard when I saw babies—especially if they were the age my children would have been. I believe in my heart that the only way you can deal with that is through Jesus. He is the ultimate ingredient in this grace, and what I did requires the ultimate in grace and forgiveness."

1. When you think of abortion, what comes to your mind?

2. It was the sound of the vacuum that stuck with Whitney for years, haunting her. Is there a particular image, sound, or memory associated with your secret that haunts you? Spend a few minutes talking to God about what is haunting you. Ask God to help you release that memory and to heal you from the pain.

3. Whitney said she wished she told someone. Are you carrying the secret of aborting a baby? If so, what is one small step you can take to share your secret?

4. Do you know someone who is carrying the secret of abortion? How can you help that person to take steps toward healing?

CHAPTER FOUR

MATT
A SURVIVOR OF PORN ADDICTION

Matt is truly one-of-a-kind, with an ability to make you feel like you're the most important person in the world. He is an encourager and a leader who seeks to make a difference in the world by candidly telling about a common struggle that 1 out of 5 men and 1 out of 8 women share. He exposes his secret in an honest, open, and straightforward way that makes others want to share their own struggles. We hope his story will spur you on. Here's Matt...

"Sparky" was the perfect childhood nickname for Matt. He was a hyper, talkative boy who was home-schooled, and his constant energy was sometimes difficult for other kids to handle. He didn't have a lot of good friends and tended to get picked on quite a bit. Yet Matt still considered himself a happy kid who loved life. Adults told him he'd be an architect one day, because he was always building and inventing things.

As an only child, Matt received a lot of attention. His parents were very protective. "Although I know my parents loved me, I had a hard time seeing that as a kid. My parents didn't allow me to make any decisions for myself for the first several years of my life." It wasn't until he was 11 or 12 that Matt felt like he had any say in the choices in his life—even the clothes he wore.

His parents struggled to deal with Matt's constant energy. His dad's intense temper would erupt at the slightest provocation—or after a bad day at work. Although he was never hit, Matt felt hurt countless times by the words his dad would use when he was angry. And sadly, it was hard to find solace in his mom, since she was struggling with bipolar disorder and her own anger issues. Matt remembers coming home from school one day to find a hole in the wall. "My mom made up some excuse about moving furniture, but I eventually found out that she had kicked the wall in." At times, her anger was directed at him. Her words could be cutting, especially when she expressed anger or disappointment in something Matt had done. As a result, he spent much of his childhood trying to be a perfectionist, hoping not to let his mom down. But whenever he failed, he felt guilty—like he hadn't lived up to her standard. Matt struggled to cope with the pressure he felt—and it was clear he couldn't talk openly about the problem with his parents. They *were* the problem!

Matt never felt like his family was stable. In fact, he would refer to his home as "the house" because it never felt like a home to him. He recalls his family planning to take a vacation in an RV over his seventh birthday. He could hardly wait! But because his parents forgot to bring the bed sheets, they got angry, fought with each other, and went home early—making it the worst birthday he ever had.

"I was only nine years old the first time I discovered pornography," Matt says. It was accidental; he was channel surfing and his parents were outside. It shocked him, but at the same time, it lured him to want to see more. Soon Matt started masturbating with porn on a regular basis. He found it was a good outlet for his feelings of frustration, and it was something he chose to do on his own, which was freeing for him. He believed it didn't affect anyone else, so why not do it? It was more than a year before his parents ever found out.

"Pornography and masturbating became something I felt I couldn't live without," Matt recalls. He'd wait for his parents to leave the house, even if they were only walking the dog around the neighborhood, and then he'd seek out porn on the family computer and masturbate. The Internet became a special place for him, and since his parents were pretty computer illiterate, Matt didn't have to work too hard to hide the Web sites he'd been visiting. "At the time, I realized I was constantly sneaking around to do this, but I liked the release it gave me and couldn't stop myself."

As his parents learned more about the computer, Matt had to be even sneakier. "I began covering my tracks online so they wouldn't be surprised by any pop-ups that could reveal my secret." But when Matt was about 10, his secret was exposed when his mom caught him. It was a moment he will never forget. She immediately became angry, then started crying. "I felt like she was trying to manipulate me with her emotions, thinking that maybe if I saw how upset it made her that I'd stop. But I didn't."

"I WAS ONLY NINE YEARS OLD THE FIRST TIME I DISCOVERED PORNOGRAPHY,"

Surprisingly, his dad didn't flare up in anger. Instead, he was just silent. Matt felt like the silence said more than any words could have. "From that point on my dad made my life miserable—taking away friends, video games, and anything else I liked." That only gave Matt more of a reason not to tell his parents how serious the problem had become. He just had to work harder to find opportunities. He wasn't going to stop just because his parents wanted him to.

Matt's parents took away the Internet for a month after they caught him. They hid the modem, but Matt found it easily. He never took it from its hiding place, but he found comfort knowing that if he got desperate, he could get online. But instead he found other ways to feed his addiction. On Friday nights he'd go to his grandparents' house to spend the night. He'd wait until they were asleep, then he'd channel surf in hopes of finding something he could use.

His parents trusted that the month-long punishment would be enough to break the habit, so after a month, Matt was allowed to use the computer again. But when Matt was caught a second time, he lost the Internet for six months. This time, rather than just taking away the computer, his parents also sent Matt to one of the church pastors for weekly talks. His mom insisted on these meetings, hoping they would help Matt stop.

"Every week, I'd sit in the office with Jake, listening to Bible verses and lectures that were supposed to make me feel convicted," Matt recalls. But it wasn't until Jake told him directly, "Matt, you're addicted to this," that he realized he had a serious problem. The word *addicted* was far more convicting than any Bible verse he'd heard. Yet even the shock of being told he was an addict still wasn't enough to actually change Matt's behavior. He was deep into this addiction, and it would take a whole lot more than words and awareness for him to change.

When he got the Internet back for the third time, Matt's parents said that if they found out he was still looking at porn, they'd get rid of the Internet for good. In Matt's mind that meant he had to work even harder to make sure they didn't find out.

Matt knew he had a problem, though, and made a number of attempts to change. "I'd go to church, say a prayer at the altar, and commit to change—but the next day I'd be back to my old patterns." It was tough to let go of what the porn and masturbation did for him. "I felt exhilaration and a high before and during the act. It was like I was able to release all the stress and pain in my life." He could momentarily forget his bitterness toward his dad because of his anger and his mom for her bipolar blowups. But immediately after the release, he'd feel guilt. He finally realized he couldn't stop the behavior. He was, in fact, addicted to porn.

And the addiction wasn't affecting only him, like he once thought. Matt began seeing girls only as objects for his personal pleasure. While he never actually had sex with any of them, he knew his attitude toward women wasn't healthy and that it would probably cause problems in relationships as he got older. "When I saw girls, I only saw their physical features. When there weren't girls around to lust after, I went to the porn."

Matt made several efforts to stop on his own. He'd count the hours he could go without porn. He once remembers going for 99 hours. When he thinks back on that time, he realizes that during those 99 hours, he was reading the Bible and journaling every day. "I realized that when I was intentionally with God, progress was being made. But when I stopped doing those things, I went downhill again."

When Matt finally accepted that his attempts to change on his own just weren't working, he decided to let someone else help him. His mom had taken him to a psychologist to deal with his issues. It was there that he discovered an eight-step recovery program for teens who are struggling with unresolved hurt from problems like addiction, abuse, and self-injury. There, he found other people with problems as big as his, or worse. "It was helpful for me to hear other people share their struggles and their journey." He found this far more encouraging than someone just telling him to stop doing it.

As part of the recovery program, Matt started dealing with the issues behind his addiction. He realized that a lot of the unhealthy attitudes he had about girls and women were things he'd learned from his dad. He remembers how his dad would devalue women by putting them down in subtle ways. He also saw how his problems with pornography and masturbation were connected to his sense of having felt so controlled by his parents—that it had been freeing for him to make his own decisions about what he wanted to do, even when those decisions were destructive for him.

During his recovery Matt learned he was not alone. He realized that others had struggled, too...many others. He also began to rely on God more and, as he did this, he soon started healing. "One of the most important things I realized is that I was living a toxic lifestyle—it was affecting everyone and everything around me."

Matt realizes he's dealing with an addiction, so the problem will never be completely gone; it will always be a struggle for him. But with the right tools and support, he's able to handle it in a much better way. "This will be an issue for the rest of my life. But I know there is hope. And I'm thankful that I no longer carry the burden of this secret alone. I know where to go to get help. I am surviving!"

REFLECTIONS

Matt suggests a few things that were really helpful to him in getting his addiction under control. First, he memorized Bible verses—which provided power when he felt tempted. He also loves to sing—so his mom suggested singing a hymn when he is tempted. (He realizes this may be a stretch for some nonsinging types!) But Matt found singing to be a good mental distraction when his mind wants to take him somewhere he doesn't want to go. But most importantly, he recognized he could not cure his addiction alone.

1. Matt struggled to find control over something in his life because he felt no control during his childhood. Do you feel out of control? What have you tried to control in your life to help you feel like you're not powerless?

2. Be honest. Do you ever look at porn? If so, how does it affect the way you see others?

3. If you struggle with pornography and masturbation, in what kind of situations are you most vulnerable? What circumstances lead you to viewing porn? (I felt lonely on Friday night, everyone else was asleep, etc....) How can you avoid those situations?

4. If pornography is a problem for you, what's the first step you can take to get help?

CHAPTER FIVE

LEAH
A SURVIVOR OF PHYSICAL ABUSE

Leah is a gracious, kindhearted woman who gives of herself effortlessly without even thinking twice about it. She's the type of person who'd offer you the shirt off her back, but the pain and struggle she's been through will grip your heart. As you read her story, I think you'll agree we'd all be better people if we had someone like Leah in our lives.

"I will never forget the first time my dad hit me. My dad and stepmom owned a big bird that lived in a huge bird-cage that was usually covered. One day I came home from school to find the birdcage uncovered and empty and our new living room furniture torn up. When my dad walked in the door that night, I was his target. He began to hit me as I screamed, 'I didn't do it...it wasn't me!' The blows just got harder. The more I tried to explain, the worse he became toward me. Blood began to drip as I ran out of the house to my neighbors'. I had to get help! The neighbor then confronted my dad, who apologetically acknowledged that it had gotten out of hand, and explained that this wasn't the norm. But I got an even harder beating that night and was told I deserved it, and to *never* tell anyone ever, *ever* again."

At one point, Leah thought, "If I only could tell my mom—surely she would do something." So she told her mom everything. To which her mom responded, "You are exaggerating, and I'm sure you did something to deserve it!" After that, Leah stopped trusting and telling anyone. She just kept it all inside.

Leah's childhood was less than desirable. Her dad had left when her mom was only a few months pregnant with Leah. He didn't like being married and didn't want another kid—especially a girl. His promise to visit the new baby became the first of many empty promises in Leah's life. She grew and got used to his absence; after all, it was all she knew.

Growing up, Leah felt invisible. Being quiet and subdued, nearly nobody noticed her. Her mom was cold, distant, and concerned primarily with her own survival. She showed little interest in anything in

Leah's world. Even though Leah had an older brother, Rich, she almost always played by herself.

When Leah was three, her mom married Frank. The first time he met Leah, he brought her a stuffed teddy bear. She thought he would make a great dad! But his kindness didn't last long. Shortly after they married, Leah's mom got pregnant with Jeff. Together the three of them formed their own family unit separate from Leah and Rich. Frank would often remind Leah and her older brother that they were not *his* children. And her mom never spoke up or helped the situation. "Family vacations" were only meant for the three of them—mom, stepdad and Jeff. Leah and Rich were left at home with a nanny.

Living life unnoticed became the norm for Leah. When Rich was held back in school due to his learning disability, he ended up in Leah's grade. With her older brother's demanding needs, Leah quickly took on the role of being his keeper. But it wasn't all bad. In fact, she liked it. Helping Rich made her feel needed and worth something.

When she was seven years old, Leah's emotions were thrown into a whirlwind. Her biological dad suddenly showed up at the house with brand new bikes for her and Rich. Most kids would have been thrilled with the gift of a new bike, but Leah was completely confused. It had been seven years since her dad left, and his arrival raised so many questions: What did this mean? Who was this man? Why did he come now? She couldn't make any sense of it—so she didn't try. When he left, it felt like a stranger had visited, brought a gift, and quickly taken off. She tried to imagine that the visit was from some random stranger and not her father. That made it a little easier for her to bear.

Not long after her dad's visit, Leah got another surprise. Her mom and Frank decided they were moving from northern California to southern California. But before the big move, her mom called Leah and Rich in from the backyard and announced, "Pack your bags now, you are going to your visit your dad." Leah was hysterical, kicking and screaming, hoping to change her mom's mind about the visit, but it was no use. She and her brother were off to visit the stranger.

The visit was a lot of what Leah expected; they didn't spend much time with their dad at all. They were with neighbors who babysat them most of the time. For the short time she was with her dad, she felt just as she did with her mom—alone.

After the time at their dad's house, Leah and Rich had become inseparable. They went to their new house in southern California and began to make it their home. They enjoyed playing with all the neighborhood kids at the local fish farm. But the fun they had together didn't last long.

Money was tight, especially since Leah's dad didn't pay child support. Food was scarce and tensions ran high between her mom and Frank. The pressure became too much and eventually, as Rich began his teenage years, he started drinking and using drugs. Leah felt helpless. Leah remembers her mom screaming at both of them for Rich's drug abuse. It was as if Leah and Rich were the same person in her mom's mind. Leah didn't seem to have a separate identity from her brother—so if he was punished, she was, too. Leah felt like her life was totally unfair and completely out of her control.

One day Leah's mom took her dad to court to get money for child support—at least, that's what she said. Both families met at the court: Her mom and step dad, her dad and his new wife, and all three kids. "I was shocked when I discovered we were there for a custody hearing," Leah remembers. "The judge agreed to let my dad take me and my brother for a visit, which actually turned out to be permanent. I remember feeling a bit of excitement as Rich and I drove up the California coast to our dad's house in a small-town community. I was hopeful for a new start. I remember having ribs that night for the first time in my life. When we arrived at our new home I naively thought: *Finally, we're a family.*"

Within a month, Leah started school in her new community. She met John, an enthusiastic boy who befriended her. Soon they became best friends. He invited her to his Christian youth group and this became a safe outlet for Leah.

But her hopes for a normal, loving family quickly dissipated when she found that both her dad and stepmom had severe drinking problems. And her disappointment was heightened when her brother Rich was forced to live on the streets because he was not welcome in the house. That's when the hitting first started. If Rich snuck home, their dad would beat him. One night Leah watched their dad torture Rich by forcing an electrical cord down Rich's throat while screaming names at him. She began to pray Rich would not come home. "But when Rich stopped coming home, my dad's abuse turned to me. I became his new target. He would hit, punch, and belt me repeatedly until there were marks or even blood. It was all I could do to survive his fits of rage. I don't know how I did..."

"HE WOULD HIT, PUNCH, AND BELT ME REPEATEDLY UNTIL THERE WERE MARKS OR EVEN BLOOD."

As if the physical abuse wasn't enough, Leah's stepmom was often verbally abusive. She would say, "You're not my child! I hate that I am stuck with you. I never asked for this. You're ugly and fat, and I never wanted you." One night she walked into Leah's room in the middle of the night, waking her from a dead sleep. She had a hot iron in her hand, holding it up screaming, "If I could, I would burn a whole in your heart!" Leah remembers like it was yesterday. "I felt frozen inside." Even at Christmas time, there was little joy in Leah's world, as her stepmom made sure there were no gifts under the tree with Leah's name on them. Her stepmom hated Leah for being alive.

While home life was a mess, Leah found her escape at school with her best friend, John, and being on the swim team. She was a good swimmer and received praise from her friends and parents publicly. But behind closed doors, it was always different. One afternoon, after swimming, she came home with her bathing suit and sweats on. Her dad said to her, "Leah, you are getting a gut!" He told her to lay across his legs with her tummy up; if he could pinch any fat, she would get a beating. Scared to death, she lay down, and fortunately, he could pinch no fat.

There was always a disconnect between what happened in private and in public. On the day her dad turned 45, Leah yelled, "Happy 45th birthday, Dad!" while he was surrounded by friends. He smiled and waved, but when she got home, she got one of the biggest beatings he'd ever given her, just for saying his age in public. He hit her with his belt, and then a stick—hard enough to leave bruised welts. She learned to keep quiet all the time.

Leah was expected to ride her bike down to the store on Sunday mornings to pick up a can of corned beef hash. "One morning, the store was out, and when I returned home empty-handed, I got hit so hard with his belt, he pulled my clothes off. I was embarrassed and broken. I wasn't able to protect myself at all. I was beaten because the store didn't have corned beef hash.

It didn't make any sense! All I wanted was to be loved, but instead I was rejected and abused."

Leah's world was spinning out of control, and the spiral soon became even worse. When she was 15, she began to babysit for her dad's close friend, Ray, who had custody of his two young daughters. One late night Ray forced Leah to have sex. Leah felt totally numb inside and didn't tell a soul. After all, what good would it do? It would probably mean another beating.

She told her dad repeatedly that she didn't want to babysit for Ray anymore, saying she was "too busy"—but her dad forced her to go. And every time she went, Ray would ask her to have sex again, grabbing her and saying, "I know you'd like it if you would just give in to it..."

Leah's fear and insecurities only increased. She could no longer sleep in her own room for fear of her dad or stepmom breaking in. Exasperated, she called her mom and told her everything. But when her mom called her dad, Leah was severely abused with the belt once again. Mom couldn't protect her. Once again, she learned to stuff her pain down deep inside her.

One day during her junior year, Leah came home from school and found a huge moving truck outside her house. She asked her dad where they were going. Coldly, he responded, "I don't know were *you* are going, but *we* are moving...Figure it out." Just like that, Leah was left alone on the front porch with nowhere to live.

Immediately she realized she must figure something out. She was afraid to let the authorities (or anyone else) know she was living on the streets. She began spending her nights going from one friend's house to another, feeling quite proud of her solution. This seemed to work until she was called out of class one day. Stepping outside the classroom, she was met by a social worker and a police officer. Her heart raced. They asked her point blank: "Where do you live? What's your address?" She couldn't hide any longer and told them the truth.

"I REALIZED THEN THAT I NEEDED TO OPEN UP ABOUT MY SECRET TO SOMEONE WHO COULD REALLY HELP ME."

Leah thought she might return to live with her mom again. But when the social worker called her mom, Leah overheard the entire conversation. Her mom said Leah needed to stay there and finish school—basically saying she wanted nothing to do with her.

She was at the local courthouse for what seemed like hours. Fear filled her heart as she desperately prayed, "If you take care of me, I'll serve you forever. Please, God, help." The police officers walked into the room and announced they'd found her a home. Leah entered the foster care system.

Leah will never forget the first night in her new home. "There was a mom, a dad, and their two daughters. They provided a warm bed, a lovely room, and a nice dinner. As I lay in bed that night, I felt safe for the first time in my life." Hope began to stir within her.

Her new "mom" would pick Leah and her two new "sisters" up from school, and they'd sit for hours at the kitchen table talking. She would tell the girls, "There is nothing we can't talk about. I care about you." Eventually, Leah believed her and began sharing the painful secret of being severely physically and sexually abused.

At one point Leah's foster family sent her to a Christian retreat, where the topic was letting go of your past so you can live a full and abundant life. "I realized then that I needed to open up about my secret to someone who could really help me." That was when she began seeing Loraine, a licensed therapist, and her life began to take a turn for the best. "Loraine helped me realize I could become all I dreamed of. It was during this time, my confidence developed, I found a relationship with God, and living a life of purpose began to surface for the first time." But working through her tumultuous pain would take many, many years of honest and hard work.

When Leah was in her early 20s, she met David, a solid and gentle man who absolutely adored her. They married, and she soon became pregnant.

The night after their first daughter was born, she heard a knock on the door. "To my utter surprise, it was my dad. My heart pounded within me. I wondered how he'd found me, why he was there, and where in the heck he had been for so many years." She told him he couldn't come in until David got home. When David arrived, she briefly talked with her dad as he handed her a pile of papers. He wanted the rights to be the baby's grandfather. She told him this was out of the question, and politely asked him to leave—and he did.

That visit from her dad marked for Leah the beginning of the very long and arduous process of forgiving all the people who had hurt and abused her—her dad, her mom, her stepmom, and Ray, the man who sexually abused her. "It was through extending forgiveness that my hate, bitterness, and resentment eventually lifted. I was finally free from the hold it'd had on me for more than 20 years."

Today Leah and David have a loving family with three children. David's deep capacity for compassion and concern has helped Leah learn to love and be loved. She's also learned the importance of setting boundaries with her family members, which makes it possible for her to have a relationship with them today.

Leah proudly serves at her church, working in a recovery group for hurting and addicted teenagers. Weekly, she hears stories like hers and, weekly, she sees people finding freedom by sharing the secrets they've long kept hidden. She is thankful God has enabled her to use the pain she's experienced to help others.

REFLECTIONS

Leah offers the following words to others who have experienced abuse: "If there has been any abuse in your life—if someone has touched you in any unwanted way—GET HELP. It's not your fault. Don't let it continue. Get the help and support you need."

1. Leah wishes she'd told her story sooner to a trusted and caring adult and regrets holding the secret of abuse. She would have liked to trust more, but simply did not know how. Do you have someone you can talk to about your secret? Someone who is older and more mature—someone you can trust? If not, call out to God, as you understand him—scream if you need to—asking that he would bring someone into your life whom you can trust.

2. Is there something you can do to help get the healing you need? Have you exhausted all your options more than once? (Counseling, journaling, recovery groups, church, etc.) What else could you try?

3. How do you see yourself today? What words would you use to describe the person you see as you look into the mirror? Write down your thoughts.

4. Look at your response to question 3. As you consider the words you've used to describe yourself, whose voice do you hear? Who described you like this? Is this description based in the truth—that you are a beloved child of God—or is it based on something else you've been told, felt, or experienced? Write down your thoughts. You may want to take a piece of paper and write a line down the middle. On one side write down the lies you've believed; on the other write down the truth of who God says you are.

Leah offers these thoughts as you pursue your own healing:

- *Don't stop with the first person you tell if they do not help.*
- *Do whatever it takes to get help.*
- *Believe you are worth it...you are. And you, too, can become a Secret Survivor.*

CHAPTER SIX

JESSICA
A SURVIVOR OF INCEST

Jessica is the kind of person others like to be around. Although she's experienced pain that has run deep into her heart and soul, she has become a stronger and more confident woman as she's become a survivor. As a mom and a writer, Jess reminds us that no matter what we encounter in life, with love and support, anything is possible. Here's our warm and lovely friend, Jessica—a survivor of incest.

Jessica sat in her counselor's office, holding her fiancé's hand as they waited. Her stomach did flip-flops as she studied the cheap, pastel-colored art on the walls of the small room. This was the day she'd been working toward for years, yet she still didn't feel ready. When her parents walked into the room, followed by her counselor, her stomach began to turn even faster. After a brief explanation from the counselor, Jessica finally spoke the secret she'd been hiding from her family for more than four years: "I was raped by my uncle when I was 17."

She watched her parents' faces drop and saw the tears begin to stream from their eyes. She saw flashes of anger cross the faces of both her dad and stepdad, while her mom melted into a puddle of tears. Jessica clung to Mark's hand and felt a strange sense of relief intertwined with the shame, regret, and leftover fear. She knew in that moment that her parents still loved her. They weren't mad at her. In fact, they said they were heartbroken that she'd carried the secret by herself for so long. On that day Jessica went from being a victim to becoming a survivor.

From the time she was a little girl, Jessica always tried to make people happy. Whether that meant cleaning the house for her mom or going to church with her dad, she hated to disappoint people. She was close with most of her family—even the aunts, uncles, cousins, and grandparents who lived all across the country. Her parents divorced when she was nine. It was a difficult time for her, but as the oldest of three children, she felt she had to be strong. She even played the role of substitute mom (when her mom had to go back to work full-time).

Jessica's mom eventually remarried, but there was still a lot of chaos in her family. Her parents' unhappiness fueled Jessica's need for their love and approval. She did everything she could to make sure her mom and dad were happy, even if their sadness had nothing to do with her. "I never wanted to add to their pain," she remembers, "so when I was going through a hard time, I kept it to myself." That's why she couldn't imagine telling her parents she'd been raped. She was already hurting enough—she didn't want to make anyone else hurt as well.

Growing up, Jessica worked hard to get good grades and stay out of trouble, but she developed a nasty habit of lying to her parents. In the beginning it didn't seem so bad, but as she entered junior high, and especially high school, her lies became a little bigger. She wouldn't mention if she'd watched an R-rated movie at her friend's house, or she'd casually lie about whether a friend's parents would be home on the night of the party she wanted to attend. Even after she became a Christian in seventh grade, Jessica struggled to be completely honest with her parents, because she never wanted them to be disappointed in her.

Jessica had decided when she became a Christian that she would wait until she was married to have sex. However, with her first serious boyfriend, Jess lost her virginity at 16. "Mike seemed so special. And he insisted we'd get married eventually, so it wouldn't really matter if we had sex. So we did," Jess shares. But they didn't get married. They broke up the summer before their senior year. But since Jessica had ditched all her friends when she started dating Mike, she felt very disconnected from anyone. So she reached out for any friendship she could find, no matter what it required of her. She "dated" a bunch of guys, but really just for the sex. Of course, for her the sex meant something else—it meant love, affection, attention, and approval. Even though she was feeling empty on the inside, she felt close to someone for a few minutes every now and then.

When Jessica was 17 her grandma was dying. So Jessica's mom and stepdad packed her and her brothers into the car for a two-day road trip to see her grandma once more and be there for the funeral. When they arrived at her grandparents' house, they decided it'd be best if Jessica and her brothers stayed with her uncle, Pete, so her grandpa and mom could deal with the pain and grief, and plan the funeral.

Pete was only nine years older than Jessica. Her first memories of him were from Christmases when she was a little girl, and he was still a kid. When Pete was in high school, he'd take her to the pool during summer visits, or bring her to the basketball court where he'd meet his friends for a late afternoon game.

Being there as Pete's mother was dying didn't seem strange to Jessica. Pete was married and had two little kids who were about one and three, and Jessica was excited to have a chance to spend some time with her cousins and her aunt and uncle. They were there only a day or two before her grandma died.

Jessica liked being around Pete because he let her be an adult. She had started smoking earlier that year but hadn't told her parents. (They smoked, too, so they never noticed the smell of cigarettes on her clothes or her hair.) "At one point he handed me the keys to his car and a pack of cigarettes, and asked if I'd run out to the store for him," she recalls. Jess basked in her freedom as she inhaled the Marlboro and drove around the small town. With the music blaring from the speakers, she felt a strange sense of confidence and independence.

EVEN THOUGH IT SEEMED WRONG TO HEAR THOSE WORDS FROM HER UNCLE, THERE WAS A PART OF HER DEEP DOWN THAT FELT GOOD.

That night her aunt had to work—at least, that's what Jess thinks she remembers. It gets a little fuzzy for her at this point, and the memories seem to come in waves. Jessica and her brothers were sleeping on couches in the living room while they stayed at Uncle Pete's house, and after her brothers fell asleep she and her uncle watched MTV. He brought her a beer. Jessica didn't really like the taste of beer, but she drank it, just like she did at the parties she went to. He handed her a cigarette and they smoked and talked as the videos played in the background.

Everything seemed fine until Pete started asking questions that seemed a little too private. "Are you still a virgin?" Jessica answered shyly, a little embarrassed to be telling her uncle about her sex life. "How many guys have you slept with?" Then he stopped asking questions and started giving her compliments. "You're really beautiful...You've got a great body...You really look older than you are..." Jessica didn't quite know how to respond. Even though it seemed wrong to hear those words from her uncle, there was a part of her deep down that felt good.

After Uncle Pete grabbed another couple of beers, he invited Jessica into the front room so he could play a song for her. She stood near the giant terrarium, looking at the iguana staring back at her, and feeling a little exposed in her nightgown. Uncle Pete put one of his favorite songs on the stereo, reminding Jessica he was definitely older than her. "Paradise by the Dashboard Lights" was a song by Meat Loaf, whom Jessica had never heard of. The song was about a young couple having sex in a car. She couldn't understand why Uncle Pete liked such a stupid song.

She was about to mock his taste in music, when her uncle came over and kissed her. Jessica pulled away, and he apologized. He began to talk some more, and Jessica really doesn't remember how it happened anymore, but at some point he coerced her to have sex with him. Jessica lost all feeling in her body and her mind went numb—except for her fear that her brothers might walk in and the haunting feeling that her dead grandma was seeing what he was making her do.

The next few days are a blur for Jessica. The funeral happened, and she cried. But she cried for more than just her grandma. After the funeral everyone went to her grandparents' house for lunch. Uncle Pete asked Jess to go for a walk with him. She declined, but he persisted, so she finally gave in—again. They walked to the park around the block, and then into the woods nearby. She can't remember what he said, but she knows he was trying to make sure their secret would remain a secret. "I was too afraid to tell anyone—especially since my grandma just died. I didn't want to add to anyone's pain, and I certainly didn't want anyone to know what I'd done." She agreed to keep their secret, and he leaned in to kiss her again. A knot began to grow in her stomach as she fought back the vomit.

The funeral was a nice excuse for Jessica's pain and grief. Everyone just assumed she was sad and depressed because her grandma had died. Her parents didn't think anything of her long face or her silence on the long drive home. Meanwhile, Jess tried to figure out what had happened to her, and why she'd let it happen.

Once she got home she thought she'd be able to move on. But Pete wouldn't let her. Her uncle began to obsess about her. He called Jessica's phone on a regular basis. A few times she answered, but then she started letting the calls go to voice mail. His messages were bizarre, rambling about moving away together and the things he'd buy for her. Jessica just hit "delete" each time, shoving the memory and the pain deeper inside.

"I felt disgusting and completely alone," Jessica remembers. "I wanted to tell someone, but I was afraid of what people would think of me. After all, it's not like he'd held a gun to my head or anything." Pete had controlled her by pure manipulation and emotional bondage. She couldn't help but feel like she had somehow "let it happen," although she knew in her gut it was the worst moment of her life—and she certainly would not have chosen for it to happen.

During the next few months Jessica tried to tell a few people about what happened. She tried to talk to her friend Rebecca one night as they drove to a party. "My uncle was really weird when I was out there. He tried to kiss me." Jess thought she'd just ease into it and see what kind of response she got. Unfortunately, Rebecca replied with, "Oh really? I think Shauna's uncle did more than that with her, but I think she liked it." Immediately Jessica knew she couldn't tell Rebecca. She knew judgment would follow, and she couldn't bear that. Eventually she decided to tell Mike, her former boyfriend—the guy she'd lost her virginity to. She pulled him into a meeting room at school one day and said, "My uncle made me have sex with him." Mike lost it. He started bawling. He looked broken. And while

Jess was touched by his grief on her behalf, she was disturbed that it affected him so deeply. His reaction made her think that her parents (and especially her grandpa) would die if she told them.

As Jessica carried this shame inside, the anger began to eat away at her. Eventually Pete stopped calling, but she couldn't stop thinking about what she'd done—what he convinced her to do. She sat at her dad's computer one Saturday and plotted how she'd kill Pete. She did it in French (she was in her fourth year)—that way no one else would know what she was typing. She wrote about how she'd wait until her aunt finally realized what a slime Pete was and moved away—that way she'd be sure her aunt and her cousins wouldn't get in the way or get hurt. Jessica thought about the creepy guy she always saw in the library at school, the one who read *The Satanic Bible,* and decided he was a big enough loser that she could pay him to kill Pete for her. It felt good to get her hatred out on paper, even if it was only a fantasy.

JESS STARTED GOING TO A COUNSELOR IN THE HOPES SHE'D EVENTUALLY BE ABLE TO TELL HER PARENTS WHAT HAD HAPPENED.

The rest of her senior year was a blur of random guys she hooked up with. The emptiness that was inside her even before her grandma died—before the rape—had grown into a vast hole inside her, and she kept looking to guys to fill that hole. She drank way too much and became an angry person. Her parents finally started catching her in some of her lies. They were really disappointed and surprised when they found out she was drinking and smoking. But she didn't care anymore. She spent the rest of the year rebelling against everyone and everything. But she knew something was wrong. She knew she needed God, even though she'd lost trust in him for letting all this happen to her.

One Sunday morning she was supposed to meet her dad at church. She'd been partying all night and was completely hung over as she drove to meet him. She really didn't want to go, but felt like she had to. That morning, in the church bulletin, she saw an announcement that the church camp was hiring summer staff. Jess had become a Christian at that camp in junior high. She felt like this was God giving her a chance to come back to him—maybe her last chance—so she applied. She barely got the job. The camp directors had a bad feeling about her, but she later learned that each year the camp would hire some kid as their "project"—a kid they thought was "on the edge" but might get back on track with God at camp. Jessica was one of those projects that summer.

Jess was excited to go to camp, but she was even more excited to get away from her family and her life. She'd be going away to college in the fall, but this would get her out of the house even sooner. She had to quit a lot of things before she went to camp. So the day before she left, she had sex one last time. On the drive to the church, she smoked her last cigarette. She was hoping to leave all that stuff behind forever—along with her pain and her secrets.

But she realized on her first night there that Christian guys were not necessarily better than other guys. Her painful past seemed to be a magnet for predators. That first night, as the staff got to know each other, everyone sat around talking late into the night. Scott stayed up late with Jessica, talking about life. Once everyone else had gone to bed, he started telling her all his deepest secrets—how many times he'd had sex, pregnancy scares, and more. Then he asked her, "So what about you? What kind of secrets do you have?" Jessica wasn't sure why, but Scott made her feel safe. She told him about all the guys, but not her uncle, and he suggested it'd be good for them to hold each other accountable that summer, since they'd have some of the same struggles. Jessica thought this made sense. But as they walked back to the cabins in the dark night, Scott turned off the flashlight and kissed Jessica. She asked him what he was doing, and he tried to convince her to go back to the lodge with him to have sex. "I was floored. I couldn't believe that after all that talk he just wanted to have sex." She was proud of herself for telling him no. She avoided Scott the rest of the summer, especially after she found out more of his secrets—like the other girl on staff he'd tried to seduce at a lifeguard training camp. Jessica had never been so relieved she'd said no.

But she met another guy that summer at camp—the man she'd eventually marry. "Mark was one of the nicest guys I'd ever met, and he was genuine." They talked all the time, and when she told him about her uncle, the compassion in his eyes was unlike anything she'd seen before. He would pray for her and write her notes telling her how special she was. She was in love before they'd been "dating" for a week. By the end of the month they knew they'd get married one day.

Jessica ended up moving back home after a single semester away at school. She wanted to be closer to Mark, and, strangely enough, she wanted to be near her family. God had softened her heart toward them while she was at camp, and she really wanted to be around them. While Jess and Mark were dating, Jessica's mom told her that Uncle Pete had developed testicular cancer. Jessica felt like God was getting back at Pete. But to her disappointment, Pete didn't die.

Jessica was still trying to heal from the pain she held deep inside. When she and Mark decided to get married, they decided Jess needed to tell her family about what her uncle had done. They both wanted to make sure Jessica was as healthy as she could be before they got married, so their marriage could be healthy as well. That's when Jess started going to a counselor in the hopes she'd eventually be able to tell her parents what had happened.

Each Tuesday afternoon Jessica would sit on a couch in the tiny office. She'd ramble on about life, school, and work, trying to avoid the topic she was paying to talk about. Each week she'd get a bigger knot in her stomach, as she knew the time was coming to tell her parents. She was scared to death. She was developing ulcers, which had probably started her senior year, but were getting worse. Every day she felt like she was about to throw up, even when she was at school or work and not thinking about Pete.

Jessica remembers freaking out a little when she heard that her aunt had left her uncle. She flashed back to her French death plot and the satanic guy at school. There was still a part of her that wanted to fulfill her evil plan, but God kept prodding her to move forward, not backward.

Even after a year of counseling, Jessica couldn't say rape. She'd say, "My uncle made me have sex with him." In her mind *rape* involved violence or force. And she still felt like she "let it happen." Her guilt and shame felt unbearable at times. But she pressed on toward her goal of telling her parents, even as she pushed aside the portion of the counseling focused on her own healing.

Her parents had no idea what was about to hit them on the day when Jess invited them to join her and Mark in the counselor's office. She'd led them to believe she'd been going to counseling for issues about their divorce. As Mark sat next to Jessica on the couch, she told her parents the hardest thing she'd ever said. As the words fell out of her mouth, she saw her parents' hearts break right in front of her.

Jess told her mom to let her sisters know what had happened—since they had daughters who lived near Pete, and Jess didn't want the same thing to happen to any of them. But she asked her parents not to tell anyone else, especially her grandpa. She also told them she didn't want to talk about it anymore. "I've been talking about it for a year in this office. I'm done talking about it. So please don't ask me questions, don't talk to me about it. Deal with it on your own." It was selfish of Jessica, and she now wishes her counselor had advised her and her parents differently. Her parents walked around on eggshells for the next few months. Occasionally Jessica would see one of them start to tear up while looking at her. But she didn't want to feel the pain anymore, so she would just walk away.

As time went on, Jessica tried to forgive Pete, since that was the "Christian" thing to do. She read books and attended seminars on forgiveness, which just made her feel guiltier because she couldn't figure out how to do it. She felt like a bad Christian, like there was something wrong with her. Even though she was trying to deal with her past, depression sank in after she and Mark had been married a couple of years. It wasn't until she started taking antidepressants that she was really able to start healing from her pain. It was around then that she was finally able to tell anyone that she'd been raped by her uncle. But as she began talking about it with friends, she found she was not so alone. There were a lot of people in her life who had suffered some kind of abuse.

Of course, Jessica had heard Romans 8:28 quoted a million times. "And we know that God causes *everything* to work together for the good of those who love God and are called according to his purpose for them" (NLT, emphasis added). But she still couldn't see how God could bring any good from her experience of being raped.

Now that she's on her journey as a survivor, some of Jessica's closest friends are people who share her pain. When she's opened up and shared her story, she's found others who have suffered hurt and abuse. She's found other people who are on a journey of healing and understanding, people who are looking for love and acceptance despite their painful pasts.

Jessica says she hasn't seen Pete for years: "I haven't spoken to him—and I don't want to." But she's come to a place in her own journey where she thinks she's forgiven him. She can't point to a day or time when it happened. There's no book or three-step process that made it possible for her to forgive. She believes she's in a process; she's on a journey toward healing. She still gets sad. She still feels rage build inside her when she hears other stories of abuse. She still struggles with her self-image and her need for approval. But God has been healing her heart a little bit at a time, and she hopes that eventually the pain and shame will completely melt away.

Today, when Jessica thinks of Romans 8:28, she can glimpse how God is able to take even the very worst experiences of our lives, and use them for good. As she tells her story, Jessica hopes it will help other people who struggle with secrets not feel alone. She hopes her story will encourage others who are mired in guilt, shame, and pain to share their stories and to release the power the secrets have over their lives. She hopes other people will become survivors, because she knows the freedom that comes from no longer being a victim.

REFLECTIONS

In *The Way of the Heart*, Henri Nouwen wrote, "What we desire most is to do away with suffering by fleeing from it or finding a quick cure."

1. How do you attempt to seek a "quick cure" when you hurt or feel pain? What do you feel about taking this way out of your hurt?

2. What feelings did you experience as you read Jessica's heartfelt story?

3. Have you ever felt unsafe or uncomfortable around a family member or another adult? If so, are you able to identify what that person does (or doesn't do) to cause you to feel this way?

4. Is there a hurt, secret, or unresolved conflict in your own life? Have you considered talking to someone trusted and safe about it? If so, who would that be?

5. Jessica says her healing is an ongoing process. Can you relate to those feelings of always being in a process of healing in any particular area of your life? If so, which one(s)? How do you deal with this?

6. Jess mentioned Romans 8:28, which reads, "And we know that God causes *everything* to work together for the good of those who love God and are called according to his purpose for them" (NLT, emphasis added). Now, consider your story or the story of someone you know. How might God bring good from it?

CHAPTER SEVEN

CHUCK
A SURVIVOR OF DRUG AND ALCOHOL ABUSE

Behind every face there is a story. Chuck's riveting story builds layer upon layer, including an intense need for approval, pressure to smoke his first joint, years of drinking to please others, failed marriages (plural!), a suicide attempt, and four arrests for drunk driving. But Chuck's a man who has learned a great deal from his past failures. Today, those closest to him say he's a "gold mine," and we agree. His insight and openness will leave you a better person. Read, and you'll strike gold, too.

"Come on, Chucky...just try some," a group of guys told him. He'd refused their offers time and time again, but this time he paused and considered it: "What can it hurt? I'll just try it." Desperate for acceptance, he finally gave in.

He could justify it in his mind. It was no big deal. He liked how the pot made him feel—he was loose and funny, less self-conscious, finally able to relax. But the best part was that he suddenly had friends. Finally.

In less than a year, he had a full-blown drug and alcohol addiction. Of course, he didn't think so at the time. He was just a high school kid trying to get by. Eventually, drinking and smoking pot just didn't have the same appeal. So he tried new drugs to get a better high.

"If it gets me high, I'll do it," he'd say to anyone who offered. When he was high and drunk, nothing mattered. He wasn't concerned about getting hurt or getting caught. In fact, the only real problem was the guilt and shame he experienced when sober. So he did his best to stay high and drunk most of the time.

Of course, it wasn't always like this—*he* wasn't always like this. Chuck remembers most of his childhood with fondness. He knew his mom and dad loved him. Chuck's mom was very caring, giving, and nurturing. She simply loved and lived for Chuck and his younger sister. His dad had a quiet strength and a strong work ethic, but he didn't know how to communicate feelings. "My dad taught me that being a man meant being thick-skinned and able to suck it up when things got rough," Chuck remembers. "So that's what I tried to do."

As a young boy, Chuck was timid and insecure, always seeking approval and attention. Smaller than everyone else his age, he overcompensated by trying to make everyone laugh at any cost. And when people mocked him, he'd push the feelings of rejection aside, as if he couldn't care less.

His family's moving six times during the first eight years of his life didn't help Chuck make friends. But he found some permanence when his family moved to North Carolina, where he lived from second to eighth grade. It was there that he got really involved in church, which planted roots of hope in his newfound relationship with God and his surrounding community. His mom and dad were thrilled!

During those formative years, Chuck played lots of sports, went on adventurous family camping trips, and traveled all over the country with his church choir during Easter and summer breaks. Chuck says his life seemed pretty "normal"—he lived with his mom, dad, and sister in a nice little home. But things were far from perfect for him: "I was still a small, scrawny, little guy who felt terribly insecure." And it showed.

His insecurity only grew in fifth grade, when a girl at school threatened to beat him up. His dad had told him, "Don't you ever, ever, *ever* hit a girl...it's not the right thing to do." And because he was a rule-follower, he obeyed—even if it cost him his reputation. One cloudy afternoon, she beat him up in front of all his classmates. Humiliated and traumatized, Chuck's self-esteem and security were rocked. He was friendless, lonely, and desperate for companionship.

When Chuck was 14, his family moved to Atlanta. In Chuck's mind, this meant a new beginning in every way—a new community, a new church, a new school...new *everything*. Chuck was thrilled, certain he would find accepting friends. But his hopes faded when his new community didn't take to him very well. He walked around school carrying his Bible and evangelism tracts. The other kids at school would either run when they saw him or make fun of him—pushing him further into his familiar isolated, lonely world.

HE WAS A MASTER AT KEEPING HIS NEWFOUND LIFESTYLE A SECRET FROM HIS PARENTS AND PEOPLE AT CHURCH.

That went on for a couple of years, until one afternoon when he was walking home from school and came across some guys who usually made fun of him. They were getting high and drunk, as they did day after day. Tired of their ridicule, Chuck finally decided to accept their invitation to try pot. And try it he did—again and again and again. Within a year, he'd developed a serious alcohol and drug problem.

He was a master at keeping his newfound lifestyle a secret from his parents and people at church. But he found himself praying and partying at the same time, and eventually he just couldn't deal with his double life any more. It took too much effort. Going to church hung over got old—so he stopped going to church altogether.

Plus, he liked his new life better, since he was no longer alone. "I would get drunk before school, disguise my alcohol during school, and drink and get high after school. If I wasn't high, I was certainly thinking about the next time I could be."

By the 11th grade, he and his friends started stealing pain pills and alcohol from every house where they'd party. This became their weekend game: One person would rummage around the bathroom; another would search out the kitchen; and another the master bedroom—seeking any substance to get them high.

"My druggie friends felt comfortable to be around," Chuck recalls. "But looking back years later, I realize it wasn't real. They weren't real. Sure, they would laugh at my jokes, but I now know they were laughing *at* me, making fun *of* me for being stupid because when I got plastered, I'd often pass out. It made for good laughs the next day." Chuck wondered if they would still be his friends if he didn't use. "Deep inside, I knew the answer..."

Chuck thought he was doing a fantastic job of keeping his addiction secret from his parents. But one morning, he asked his mom why he had a big knot on his head. She told him he'd fallen down the stairs. When he asked if she'd checked on him, she said, "No, you were drunk." Chuck was surprised. That same day, his mom was vacuuming under his dresser and found a big bag of pot. When he got home from school, she told him she'd flushed it down the toilet. The secret was now out, but Chuck remembers only one time when his mom and dad confronted him about his noticeably out-of-control behavior—when they put him on restriction "until God said he could get off." (Apparently, he is still on restriction, because they never did tell him he was off!)

Looking back, Chuck knows his parents felt powerless. They just didn't know how to support him, didn't have the tools to deal with his behavior—so they ignored it. But inside, Chuck was desperate for someone to rescue him from his downward spiral. He put on such a good front that no one had a clue he was dying on the inside. "I wished I could trust my parents and share with them the depth of my problems and struggles. But my parents wouldn't understand." Chuck learned later that his parents had their own problems—their marriage was heading for divorce. Numb to his family's upheaval, Chuck kept drinking and using to bring comfort to his tattered life.

By a small miracle, Chuck made it through high school and headed off to college on a golf scholarship. His first week there, he bought 1,800 painkillers, and began downing at least 30 a day, while simultaneously drinking and smoking. Out of control, and desperately missing his girlfriend, who lived 70 miles away, Chuck dropped out of school to marry her. They were 20 years old, both lost in a world of alcoholism and loneliness. The marriage lasted six months.

After the divorce, Chuck continued using. "I was jumping from job to job, unstable and unable to stay anywhere for long." The one constant was his visits to his Grandma's house in Florida, where he could hang out at the beach and party. While barhopping there, he met a beautiful young woman. Desperate for love, they eventually got married. But like the first, this marriage lasted less than a year.

But Chuck could always pick himself up after a fall, and this second divorce was no exception. An entrepreneur at heart, he started his own business. But he was still deep in his addictive lifestyle, and was soon heavily involved with smuggling and dealing cocaine. This led to the downfall of the business.

Eventually, Chuck realized he needed help, and made the courageous step to put himself into treatment. Sadly, it didn't last; he just wasn't ready.

Before long he found himself in a relationship with a married woman. She promised she was getting a divorce and would live with him, but that was never her plan. Even though Chuck was an addict, he still had a sensitive heart—and when she played him over and over, he hit bottom for the first time: "This is a vivid memory for me. I took a sudden trip to my mom's house, and while I was there I had a doctor prescribe antidepressants for me. Even though the prescription clearly stated you should not drink alcohol while taking the antidepressants, I did anyway. As you may guess, the combination of the drugs and alcohol forced me into a deep depression. After my tenth bottle of cheap beer, I broke the glass and sliced both my wrists; blood fell everywhere."

The paramedics took Chuck to the hospital, where he was immediately put into treatment, which was a big wake-up call. "During my first three days there, I read the 700-page 'Big Book' of Alcoholics Anonymous. It felt like I was finally turning a corner. I desperately wanted to change—to be free—and I knew I needed to do *something* different."

By now, he had three DUI's on his record and he knew he had to be careful. He managed to give the hospital staff the impression that he was serious about getting better, and he was released. For a little while, he did well. He was sober for the first time in years. But again, he just wasn't ready to make the change to his life. "I just wasn't able to be honest with people, myself, or God yet."

After six months of sobriety, Chuck started drinking again. Now 25, he was certain he could control his drinking, that he could simply ease his way into it. He started his own construction business, which quickly became quite successful. But as the money was coming in, the pressures of running the business increased. Trying to cope, his drinking got out of control and he lost everything. His life seemed manageable only when he was on something. He found himself drinking morning, afternoon, and night. Sometimes, to get an extra kick, he would prepare lines of cocaine at night so he'd have something to wake up to in the morning.

HIS ABILITY TO HANDLE HIS ALCOHOL AND DRUGS TOOK A TURN FOR THE WORSE WHEN HE GOT HIS FOURTH DUI.

"I got so depressed at one point during this time that I took every pill in the house—heart pills, antihistamines—anything I could get my hands on. I overdosed and actually stopped breathing. I didn't want to die—I just wanted to get out of the prison of my addictions. But I just couldn't seem to do it. I felt powerless." His overdose put him in a coma for a week; his parents were told he would likely never come out of it. But God gave Chuck another opportunity. "One week later, I woke up from my coma. I knew this was a second chance at life and I was determined to make a difference this time."

But Chuck was still lonely and, once again, he found love in the wrong place. He met Lacy, a woman six years younger, who was living in her car with her two children. Chuck's compassion overruled his logic when he invited Lacy and her two kids to move in. The kids' dad had abandoned them, and they were desperate for a daddy. And that is what Chuck became, literally overnight. Chuck was hooked; he loved kids and had always wanted to be a father.

Although they both drank excessively and partied endlessly, Chuck still believed he was in love with Lacy and wanted them to be a family—so, they got married. And within four months, they had Dusty, a son whom Chuck loved deeply.

Chuck was sure his third marriage would last. But like all the rest, it eventually turned sour. Lacy was a very angry, aggressive woman when she was drunk. She'd attack and hit him, then would call the police and try to send him to jail. But when the alcohol wore off, she'd shower her love on Chuck once again. They were parents of a family of five, but still partying and drinking—and feeding their addictions left them unable to pay the bills. It didn't take long before they were evicted.

On their one-year anniversary, Chuck finally left his chaotic home life, taking Dusty with him. It broke his heart to leave Lacy's other kids, but he knew he had to leave her, which also meant leaving them.

With this new, but shaky, start, Chuck found hope in starting another business with a friend. He had stopped using and thought he would never use again. But Chuck's hopes were shattered when his partner cheated him out of the business, leaving Chuck with next to nothing.

Chuck's pain was compounded by the deaths of both his mom and grandma, who died right around this same time. The gaping hole in his heart was too much to take, and he went back to the bottle for comfort—living, as he would say, as a "functioning alcoholic."

But his ability to handle his alcohol and drugs took a turn for the worse, when he got his fourth DUI. He was facing up to a year in prison and the possibility of losing both his house and his son. Losing his son would be too much to bear.

Finally, he hit rock bottom, and surrendered himself completely.

Chuck pleaded with God for the first time. And by the grace of God, he says, was granted house arrest. He managed to keep his business going despite his partner's betrayal, and found a guy he could pay to drive him to and from his job. He had his business, his home, and most importantly, he had Dusty.

"After my fourth DUI, I stopped drinking, surrendered my life to God, and started going back to church, rekindling my childhood faith. For the first time in my life, I understood how much God loved me. I started going to Alcoholics Anonymous and was exposed, for the first time, to the power of God and community. That's when I started thinking more about what God *can* do and what he *would* do if I allowed him to."

For the first time since that first hit of pot nearly 20 years earlier, Chuck had a new set of eyes. Suddenly, life felt hopeful. While he knew he was in a good place, there seemed to be something missing. He looked into other programs to help him get better connected and be held more accountable. He found Celebrate Recovery, a biblically based 12-step program.

At Celebrate Recovery, Chuck found a place where he could be honest about his future while working through his past. "If I missed a church service or a Celebrate Recovery meeting, I felt like I hadn't eaten for a week!" When he was there, he felt acceptance, forgiveness, and the hope he had never found for so many years. Finally, Chuck was home.

Chuck began to pray about every decision. Knowing that Lacy's two older boys still needed a father figure, he bought two trailers nearby, one for him and one for Lacy and the boys. That way the boys could see both mom and dad on a daily basis. Conveniently, the trailers were also close to the church—so when Chuck was asked to become a leader at Celebrate Recovery, his answer was an easy "Yes!"

Chuck was finally on the road to real recovery. "I loved my new life. Loved being sober. Loved my sons. Loved God. And I loved having a purpose for my life."

Today, 12 years later, Chuck remains sober. He lives in Southern California, and is married to Mary, a beautiful Christian woman. Together they live with her daughter and Dusty. After years of rebellion and hurt, Chuck is using his secret and destructive past to help others heal. He continues as a leader at Celebrate

Recovery, and he and Mary also lead an eight-step recovery group for teenagers at their church.

Chuck's years in recovery have taught him a great deal about the power of God. "It's just amazing what God will do if we trust and believe in him," he says. "It's unbelief that keeps us from experiencing the fullness of life. The power we use is probably only a tenth of what's at our disposal through God."

REFLECTIONS:

According to Joseph A. Califano Jr. of The National Center on Addiction and Substance Abuse, people who reach age 21 without ever smoking, abusing alcohol or using drugs are "virtually certain" never to do so.

1. How can you find support for yourself and support your friends so that you and those you love stay away from paths that could lead to addiction problems in the future?

2. If you are a teenager who's struggling with the secret use of alcohol and/or drugs, Chuck would say you don't have to wait until you are an adult to heal from your problems. How could you begin to heal from your problems today? What is one small step you can take?

3. Chuck was desperate for someone to rescue him from his downward spiral. To whom could you turn for the help you need?

4. Most users are experts at hiding the reality of their addiction. Here are some signs that a person might be struggling with a substance abuse problem:
   - sudden mood change
   - grades dropping
   - change in friends
   - lack of hygiene
   - sudden weight drop or gain
   - depression
   - withdrawal
   - reckless behavior
   - lethargic
   - carelessness about the future
   - lying, disrespectful attitude especially to family members
   - running away
   - aggression
   - anger
   - forgetfulness, etc.

   If you know someone who is struggling with the secret use of alcohol and/or drugs, what could you say to him?

CHAPTER EIGHT

CATHERINE
A SURVIVOR OF AN EATING DISORDER

Catherine is a beautiful soul who once struggled with a problem that is shared by far too many young women. It's estimated that one of every four girls is battling an eating disorder—and Catherine was that one. For many years, issues surrounding eating, weight, and body image dominated her life. But today she draws on the pain of her own struggle and the inner strength she discovered to help others heal. Perhaps you'll be the next person to benefit from her story...

Early in her high school years, Catherine would eat like crazy and then exercise to work it off. "I would run miles and miles, and then get on and off the scale, sometimes two, three, or four times a day. I felt so out of control and it seemed to get worse each year. I tried it all...diet pills and fad diets began to rule my life—my every thought. It seemed to be the one area I could control."

If you'd asked her family at the time, they would have said she was very aware of her body—very self-conscious—but not someone with an eating disorder. Even as friends began to notice and express concern, she convinced herself they were wrong. "Besides, when I looked in the mirror, I truly believed I saw someone who was fat!"

When Catherine Grace was a child, her boundless energy and enthusiasm led her mom to call her "Spunky." Even as a young kid, she had a magnetic personality; friends were easy to find and easy to keep. People were always drawn to her, and she loved the attention. While she liked school and did well, she mostly focused on having fun with friends, not unlike anyone else her age. They loved to play!

But at a very young age, Catherine felt like she just didn't fit in with the rest of her family. "I knew intuitively that I was the family *oops*—that my mom hadn't intended to get pregnant a third time with me." Her energy and strong will seemed to overwhelm her parents. And it didn't help that her older sister could do no wrong by her mom, and that her older brother, the sports fanatic, was dad's favorite.

Catherine tried her best to please her parents, only to realize that nothing she could do or say could win her parents' affection and favor. Eventually she moved on, trying to get other people's approval instead. She would do just about anything to attract a look, a comment, or the applause of others—all stemming from the lack of approval she experienced from her mom and dad.

Growing up, Catherine felt like her family "lived" at church—and for the most part, she liked it. Church was where she found her closest friends, including Jeannie, her very best friend. Together, they laughed, played, and made fun of the pastor's sermons.

But there were aspects of church life that weren't as much fun. Catherine's extended family was full of pastors from a strict conservative background, which created a world of rules in which she had to live. There were the obvious spoken rules her mom and dad would repeat like, "What happens at home stays at home... don't talk to anybody about our business!" But there were also unspoken rules, such as the requirement to always appear to be the "perfect family" and the constant pressure to try to be the person her mom and dad wanted her to be—rather than the energetic fireball she really was.

Yet Catherine's mom and dad provided a home with a lot of stability. Mom stayed at home with the kids while Dad earned his living as a teacher. Each day was couched in a familiar daily regimen. But that routine changed in the summers, since her dad was off. The family grew to love summers! One summer, Catherine remembers traveling across country in the family station wagon—the three kids all in the back seat fighting, laughing, sleeping, and eating all the way there.

Her mom and dad worked hard to create lasting memories. But there are some memories Catherine wishes she could forget. She remembers struggling to feel close to her dad: "I desperately wanted to connect with my dad and for him to notice me. I painfully remember one time when we went out to lunch when he asked me, 'What grade are you in again?' He didn't have a clue! He was so detached—he often felt like a stranger living in my own home."

It wasn't just Dad's emotional absence that was hurtful for Catherine. Her mom had anger issues, and strong-willed Catherine often became the target of her anger. Her mom once got so angry she was spanking Catherine with a wooden hanger, yelling, "Cry softly... cry softly!" as Catherine tried to get away by crawling up the post on her bed.

That experience only solidified what Catherine knew she had to do—hold everything in; don't let them know how you really feel. "That's when I became an expert at wearing a mask in nearly every relationship. I often became exactly what someone else wanted me to be. I would deny who I really was and how I really felt so they would like me. This made me feel extremely insecure inside—which inevitably left its mark on everything I said, did, and thought."

Although she put on a great front, Catherine was dying inside. And that's when she began using food to bring her comfort. Growing up, her parents didn't have a lot of money. "We went shopping once a month and when we came home, I would write my name on the Pop-Tarts or candy, hoping my brother wouldn't eat it. I found myself thinking about food often, thinking I would just have one bite, but then eating all of it."

When she was about 12, she began babysitting for a nearby family. They asked her to babysit often, and she quickly grew to love being around them. They seemed like the ideal family she'd always hoped for: The mom was a former beauty queen and model; the dad was charming, accepting, loving, and fun. It appeared she'd finally found acceptance. But she became aware of the intense way that the dad, Devin, was staring at her. She felt awkward and silly around him but, in an odd way, it also made her feel good inside. "I began to crave his attention...his looks."

One night when Catherine was babysitting, during a time when the couple was having marriage problems, Devin came home after Catherine had put the kids to bed. His wife was still out, and he sat down next to her on the couch. He began to touch her leg. Then, slowly, he moved beneath her clothes while saying, "You are so beautiful...you are so mature..." She felt numb at the time. She was being touched for the first time—by an older man—in very private places. She felt so detached, thinking, "This couldn't be happen to *me*." But it was happening—and it would happen several more times.

Trying desperately to understand it all, she finally gained enough courage to tell one of her girlfriends, who simply said, "Don't tell anyone else." The next time she babysat, she mentioned to the dad that she'd said something to a friend. He became enraged, pulled the car over to the side of the road, and said, "I can't believe you did that! You can never babysit for us again!"

Catherine Grace was stunned, unable to understand what happened. After all, he'd said that he loved her, that he wished he were married to her instead of his wife. It was a devastating blow.

They never did call her to babysit again, and the violating incidents went underground. Feeling abandoned by the dad, she didn't tell another soul, keeping her shame-filled secret to herself. "Yet now I'd learned to equate 'love' with the worth of my body, and I repeated the cycle with other guys I was in relationships with for years to come."

This was when her eating became completely out of control. She had to find something to help her deal with all the pressure—her secret pains. Becoming obsessed with food, exercise, laxatives, and diet pills was her answer—at least for a while. "I was deep into what I now know was an eating disorder."

But shortly after graduating from high school, Catherine met Michael, whom she went on to marry when she was only 19. She believed she could hide her secret even from him, and she did...for a while. But one time she was in their dark garage, shoveling down a gallon of ice cream, when Michael walked in. "What are you doing?" he asked. She quickly threw the container aside hoping he hadn't noticed. But her secret was starting to unravel.

MICHAEL WOULD TELL HER OVER AND OVER: "YOU ARE SO BEAUTIFUL...YOU LOOK SO GREAT." BUT SHE SIMPLY DID NOT—COULD NOT—BELIEVE HIM.

Michael would tell her over and over: "You are so beautiful...You look so great." But she simply did not—could not—believe him. She truly thought he was lying just to pacify her—or to get her to stop asking, "Do I look fat?" In fact, she would often call him a liar. She felt so insecure. She remembers, "Whenever Michael was near another female, I felt like I could never measure up. I was fearful that he would find someone better, more beautiful, more attractive. I was deeply afraid of being rejected and left behind. That's why food was such a huge comfort. It was something I could count on. It made me feel good for the moment. It was very reliable and always available with no strings attached."

The truth was, she honestly believed her problem wasn't *that bad.* After all, she could control it, or so she thought. But the longer she held her secret inside, the more her dysfunctional relationship with food intensified. "It started out with bad self-esteem due to the pain from my parents' rejection and being molested. That led to being obsessed with people-pleasing. When I couldn't get others' approval, how I looked became an obsession. Binging and then purging through exercise, laxatives, and then eating next to nothing became a pattern. I would feel tremendous disgust and shame, but it would always cycle back again. Binging, purging, disgust, and shame—it felt like I was on a never ending treadmill."

It wasn't until she was in her early 30s and had kids that Catherine truly began to panic. Her secret was becoming more obvious and out of control, and her world was rapidly unraveling. She finally hit rock bottom and realized she had to do something more extreme. In the midst of a deep depression, she marched herself into therapy and an Overeaters Anonymous group.

But for Catherine, it would get harder before it got easier. She noticed that whenever she went to see her counselor, she'd want to stop off at a local store and eat everything in sight! Eating helped her avoid the painful reality of what was going on deep inside. After all, it was easier to eat and exercise than deal with the deeper, more painful stuff.

People in her overeaters group would tell her, "It's not about the food...it's not about the scale." But this made no sense to her—she still thought, "If only I weighed X, then I'd be fine." It wasn't until she finally came to terms with her lifetime struggle, to admit she had an eating disorder and she could no longer control it, that permanent change came.

During this time, she uncovered the reasons behind her secret—the food-and-exercise addiction—which all pointed back to the pain of feeling unwanted and unloved by her parents and being molested at an early age. This was far too much for a young child to bear, and it led to a secret struggle that would eventually rule her thoughts, her hopes, her very life! She's worked hard to unlock and strip away the lies she so deeply believed and to forgive her parents and the man who molested her.

As a mom, Catherine was forced to realize that nearly everything she's believed about herself was getting transferred to her daughter, Sarah. Sadly, Sarah began to develop her own eating disorder, partly because of her mom's unresolved pain, which transferred to her. While Sarah is still not out of the woods, together she and Catherine have worked hard to see themselves and each other as precious, fragile people who are deeply loved.

Catherine reflects, "Today, I am a survivor—not only from an eating disorder, but also from the scale, my jeans size, the mirror, and what others see. I'm so much more at peace with who I am. I work hard not to abuse my body. My goal is to be healthy and take care of myself. I no longer see food as 'all good' or 'all bad' and have learned to be kind to myself—to love who I am and be at rest internally." She is more integrated, seeing her body not as the sum of all she is, but as one part of the whole person.

"I think our secrets will stick with us until we are willing to face them and get honest about the question, 'What is the root of the pain?'" But once someone answers that question, they are on their way toward healing.

Catherine Grace attributes her own healing to wise counsel, to getting into a support group where she was not judged, and to Jesus Christ, who helped lift her burden of pain. Furthermore, forgiveness, restoration, and healing have taken place with her own parents. Her past is behind her, yet it's also being used for something greater. For the last five years, she has led a small group of junior high and high school students in an eight-step recovery group for teens with pain and addiction. She's found that eating disorders are among the issues she most often finds herself helping students deal with. Today, she is using her once-secret pain to help others heal and become survivors themselves.

REFLECTIONS

While many persons with an eating disorder are very good at hiding the problem, some signs of a possible eating disorder include excessive exercise, trips to the bathroom immediately following a meal, obsessing about one's body, and a pattern of eating a great deal at some meals and skipping others.

1. Do you or someone you know have an eating disorder? If so, find someone older whom you can trust, and tell that person honestly about the problem—so you or your friend can get the support you need.

2. How do you use food or exercise as comfort?

3. What do you see when you look in the mirror? Is your answer based on what someone told you or what you really know to be true?

4. If you engage in an eating disorder or other coping behaviors, have you ever tried to get to the root of your pain? What is it? What small steps can you begin to take toward taking care of yourself and to start healing?

SHARING YOUR SECRET

HOW TO WRITE YOUR SURVIVOR STORY

There is no magic formula to being a survivor of your secret. But we have found that by telling someone else about whatever it is you're hiding, you can begin the journey to healing and surviving.

It's not easy to take that first step of sharing your secret with someone else. For many survivors, it takes years before they are willing to open up to someone and begin the healing journey. Sometimes you can take a step in that direction by writing down your story. We'd like to suggest a couple of options for how you might do that.

In some cases, you may want to write out your secret in the form of a letter to the person or persons who hurt you. You don't necessarily have to send the letter you write. This process can be valuable even if you never send it—even if it's impossible to send it because the person you are writing to has died or is no longer a part of your life.

When I (Megan), first went to counseling, my therapist suggested I write such a letter. At first it felt daunting. I didn't mail the first letter I wrote—I'd poured out so many feelings that I felt like I'd emotionally thrown up all over it! But venting all those emotions was an important part of the healing process for me. I eventually decided to write a less angry letter (although there was still some anger in it)—which I did send.

Writing my feelings by addressing the four issues below was tremendously helpful in my healing process:

1. This is what happened (recall the details of the event).
2. This is how I felt at that time (relive how you felt during the trauma).
3. This is how it has affected my life (remember its mark on your life to date).
4. This is what I want from you now (release the person from the hold on your life).

In some situations it may feel more appropriate and effective to write your secret out as a story. The steps below can help you write your own story in a simple, straightforward way. Sometimes, it's easier to tell the story as a narrator, as if you are describing someone else's experience, rather than speaking from your own perspective as the main character. This can help you step outside the pain for a bit and look at it through a different lens. It allows you to tell your secret in a way that's a bit less personal while still allowing you to process through the events and the pain.

Writing your story gives you the courage to take the first step of sharing your secret and beginning your healing journey. Here are the steps you can take to get started:

1. Choose a different name for yourself as well as for the main characters in your story. This helps you remove yourself a little from the story, and allows you to maintain anonymity while you're working up the courage to share your secret.

2. Start with your childhood:
    a. What were you like as a little kid?
    b. How would your parents describe you?
    c. Whom did you play with? What kinds of things did you do with your friends?
    d. What were your dreams?
    e. What are your favorite childhood memories?
    f. What painful childhood memories do you carry?

3. Move into your teenage years:
    a. How have you changed since you were a little kid?
    b. When did you first realize you were changing?

c. What people, places, choices, or events contributed to changes in you?

d. What is your relationship with your parents like now?

e. Who are your closest friends?

f. What are your future plans?

4. Incorporate your secret into the story. This may be something that fits into the childhood portion of your story, or it may be more recent. Use as many details as you can remember to help you paint the picture of the secret:

   a. What is your secret(s)?

   b. If it was something done to you, describe what happened...Where were you? Who was there? How did it happen? How did you feel after it happened?

   c. If it was something you did, describe what happened. If it's something you've done more than once, start by talking about the first time. What did you do? Why did you do it? How did you feel after it happened?

   d. What did you do after your secret became part of your story?

   e. Did you try to tell anyone? If so, who? What was that person's reaction? How did that make you feel?

f. If you've never told anyone, why not?

g. How has your secret affected who you are today?

h. How has your secret affected your relationships with your family and friends?

i. How has your secret affected your view of God?

5. The next chapter of your story...We hope you can write this part into your story after you've told someone your secret and begun your journey to healing.

   a. Whom did you tell?

   b. Why did you choose to tell that person?

   c. How did that person react?

   d. How did it make you feel to finally let go of your secret?

   e. What is different about you now that you've released your secret?

   f. How do you think your story could help other people who are dealing with a similar issue?

   g. What are you going to do now?

After you've written all the pieces of your story, you may want to rearrange the order of it. You might want to start with the secret, or you may want to begin with your childhood. It's not important if the story is well written or even if it's presented in a logical order. The point is to get it out on paper so that you can begin to feel comfortable enough with it that you'll be able to share your story with someone else.

If you need a place to start, you can tell your story at SecretSurvivors.com. It'll be good practice for you to prepare to tell a person you trust—such as a parent, a counselor, or a pastor. And we'll be there to pray for you and encourage you as you take those next steps toward healing and becoming a Secret Survivor.

WHERE WAS GOD?

Like many survivors, we wrestled with many questions during our struggle—and those questions grew even larger as we began to confront the pain in our past and started to heal. One of the biggest questions (and one of the hardest ones to answer) is "Why did God allow this to happen?"

I (Jen) remember going to a seminar about healing at a Christian conference while I was in college. It was led by two counselors who had written a book about dealing with pain and trauma in our lives. I figured it would be a good event for me to attend, in hopes that these experts would be able to help me heal. This was still a few years before I'd be able to share my secret with others, so I was still very raw.

During the seminar, the counselors asked those of us who were struggling to heal from a painful or traumatic experience to stand up. I stood, and saw I was surrounded by about a thousand other people my age who were also dealing with some kind of pain. The speaker said, "Now, close your eyes and replay in your mind the painful experience you had." I closed my eyes and reluctantly replayed my experience. After a few minutes you could hear sniffles around the room as people started to feel the pain of their memories. Then the speaker said, "Now, I want you to replay the experience again. But this time, I want you to look for Jesus... because he was there. He's always with us."

I closed my eyes and wondered where I could find Jesus in my story. I couldn't imagine he was actually there during the most awful experience of my life. But as I replayed my story, I noticed Jesus sitting in the corner of the room. He was crying. I broke down crying, myself.

I sat down and wept, like countless other people in the room. I don't remember what the speaker said during the rest of the workshop, because I spent the rest of that time (and the next several years) wondering to myself: If Jesus was there, why didn't he do anything? If he's so powerful, why would he just sit there crying like a helpless bystander? If he was there, and if he really loves me, why didn't he stop it from happening?

Every Christian who has experienced something painful has asked that question at some point. Why would God allow this to happen? Why did God just sit there?

I wish I had an easy answer to these questions. But I don't. There are no easy answers to questions like these. Sometimes there are things in life we will never fully understand, and we just have to come to a point of accepting them despite the lack of clarity. God gives us all freedom to make our own decisions—and the tragic truth is that people often make destructive choices that bring untold suffering to themselves and others. And I believe that, when we suffer because of choices we and others have made, God cries with us.

I have struggled for years to understand who Jesus really is because of that exercise in the seminar. I had a difficult time truly believing that God is all-powerful and that he loves me. Sometimes I still wrestle with that. But I have come to accept that Jesus does love me. I can't explain why God lets bad things happen to any of us, and I don't know anyone who has a good explanation (although some people may try to offer you a Bible verse or two that explains it). Deep in our hearts, when we've been hurt so badly, words don't always mean much.

We're not going to give you a bunch of Bible verses to try to convince you God was there and that he wants to bring something good out of the pain you've experienced (even though those things are true). We know that those words often sound hollow when the pain is eating you up inside. But we do want to remind you that many of the people in the Bible suffered great pain and loss, just as you have. We mention these people not because they are all perfect examples of how best to deal with pain, but because they are all humans who experienced great pain and allowed God to heal and use them in spite of that pain.

You've probably heard about the shepherd boy David who battled Goliath and eventually became king. But you may not know that King David later had an affair with a married woman and then, in an attempt to cover it up, sent her husband to the front lines so he'd be killed! Yet because of his repentant and willing spirit, God called David "a man after [my] own heart." (1 Samuel 13:14).

Joseph was shown such extreme favor by his dad that, as a result, he was hated, abused, and left for dead by his brothers. He later became second in command in all of Egypt, and eventually forgave his brothers saying, "You intended to harm me...God intended it for good" (Genesis 50:20).

Jeremiah suffered from depression; the Samaritan woman had several failed marriages; Samson was codependent; Rahab was a prostitute; Elijah was suicidal—and many, many more. The point is that all these biblical heroes experienced pain—sometimes it was because of something they'd done; sometimes it was because of something done to them; and sometimes it was a mixture of both. Yet God used each of them to impact lives. You see, nobody has a perfect story. We are all flawed. We all carry secrets. You are not alone. Everybody hurts.

We'd like to invite you to use the space on the next few pages to work through some of your own pain, frustration, and questions for God. We hope you'll use the space provided to write or draw your responses to the questions or prompts. Allow your true feelings and thoughts to come out—don't worry about hurting God's feelings. You are allowed to be angry with God. You're allowed to question his actions (or his inaction). He is big enough to handle how you feel.

Remember...be honest. Let your feelings come through on the following pages, and pour your heart out. Take as much time and space as you need—you can write your answers on a separate piece of paper if you prefer. Feel free to answer only the questions that apply to you, and skip those that don't:

- How did you view God before your secret was part of your life?

- How did your secret change your view of God?

- Where do you think God was in the midst of your painful experience?

- How do you feel about the fact that God allowed you to experience this pain?

- What do you want to say to God? What do you want to tell him about the pain you're feeling now? Remember, you can't hurt his feelings—so be honest.

- Does it help you to know that God was there in the midst of your painful experience? Why or why not?

- What do you wish God would have done? If you were God, what would you have done?

- Are you willing to ask God to heal you from your hurt? Why or why not?

- What is your heart's prayer? What is it you most desperately want from God now? What would an answer to that prayer look like?

We suggest you take the time to write your heart's prayer in a journal or on a separate piece of paper and put it someplace safe. Pray these words every day for the next month; then come back and think through these questions again. How has a month of praying your heart's prayer changed things? What has changed in your heart? How has God changed for you?

We hope this exercise helps you process some of the pain and questions you have for God. Dealing with these feelings is a necessary step on your journey to become healthy and whole again. Congratulations! You're on your way to becoming a Secret Survivor.

ADDITIONAL RESOURCES

General Recovery and Support

Secret Survivors

www.secretsurvivors.com

Celebrate Recovery
(12-step biblical recovery program for adults)

www.celebraterecovery.com

Life Hurts, God Heals
(8-step biblical recovery program for teenagers)

www.lifehurtsgodheals.com

Heart Support

www.heartsupport.com

To Write Love on Her Arms

www.twloha.com

Focus Adolescent Services

www.focusas.com

Alcohol and Drug Abuse

Center for Substance Abuse Treatment
www.csat.samhsa.gov
800-662-HELP

Al-Anon/Alateen (for family members of person with addictions)
www.al-anon.alateen.org
888-4AL-ANON

Alternatives in Treatment
www.drughelp.com
800-622-0866

Alcoholics Anonymous
www.alcoholics-anonymous.org
212-870-3400

National Institute on Drug Abuse
www.drugabuse.gov
301-443-1124

Crystal Meth Anonymous
www.crystalmeth.org
213-488-4455

StreetDrugs.org
www.streetdrugs.org
763-473-0646

Self-Injury

Psyke

www.psyke.org

Self-Abuse Finally Ends (S.A.F.E. Alternatives)

www.selfinjury.com

1 800-DONT CUT

Young People and Self-Harm

www.selfharm.org.uk

Self-Injury Meetup

self-injury.meetup.com

Rape, Incest, and Sexual Abuse

Rape, Abuse & Incest National Network

www.rainn.org

800-656-4673 (HOPE)

Hope for Healing

www.hopeforhealing.org

Pornography and Sexual Addictions

Pornography Overcomers Outreach
www.overcomersoutreach.com
1 800-310-3001

XXXChurch (pornography accountability)
www.xxxchurch.com
616-588-5988

Be Broken Ministries
www.bebroken.com
800-49-PURITY

Kickporn
www.kickporn.com

Eating Disorders

National Bulimia/Anorexia Self-Help Hotline

800-227-4785

National Eating Disorders Association

www.nationaleatingdisorders.org

800-931-2237

National Association of Anorexia Nervosa and Associated Disorders

www.anad.org

1 847-831-3438

Mirror Mirror

www.mirror-mirror.org

TeensHealth

www.kidshealth.org/teen

Abortion

After Abortion

www.afterabortion.com

Safe Haven Ministries

www.safehavenministries.com

Project Voice

(A place to share your story with others who have had abortions)

www.theabortionproject.org

Physical and Emotional Abuse

National Teen Dating Abuse Helpline

www.loveisrespect.org

866-331-9474 or 866-331-8453 (TTY)

ChildhelpUSA Child Abuse Hotline

www.childhelp.org

800-4-A-Child

National Domestic Violence/Abuse Hotline

800-799-SAFE (7233)

www.ndvh.org

800-787-3224 TTY

Residential Treatment Centers

General Information

www.residentialtreatment-centers.com

800-303-0516

Aspen Ranch (Utah)

www.aspenranch.com

877-231-0734

The Canyon

www.thecyn.com (California)

877-345-3396

Books for Teens

Crossroads: The Teenage Girl's Guide to Emotional Wounds by Stephanie Smith and Suzy Weibel (Zondervan, 2008)

How to Help Your Hurting Friend by Susie Shellenberger (Zondervan, 2004)

Cutting by Steven Levenkron (W. W. Norton, 1998)

Cut: Mercy for Self-Harm by Nancy Alcorn (Winepress, 2007)

Starved: Mercy for Eating Disorders by Nancy Alcorn (Winepress, 2007)

Let Your Life Speak by Parker Palmer (Jossey-Bass, 2000)

Messy Spirituality by Mike Yaconelli (Zondervan, 2002)

Love Beyond Reason by John Ortberg (Zondervan, 1998)

Posers, Fakers, & Wannabes by Brennan Manning and Jim Hancock (Navpress, 2003)

Books for Adults

Hurt: Inside the World of Today's Teenagers by Chap Clark (Baker, 2004)

Reviving Ophelia by Mary Pipher (Ballantine Books, 1994)

Your Adolescent by David Pruitt (HarperCollins, 1999)

Disturbing Behavior by Lee Vukich and Steve Vandegriff (AMG Publishers, 2005)

Help Your Teenager Beat an Eating Disorder by James Lock and Daniel le Grange (Guilford Press, 2005)

Addiction & Recovery for Dummies by Brian Shaw, Paul Ritvo, Jane Irvine, and M. David Lewis (Wiley Publishing, 2005)

Hope and Healing for Kids Who Cut by Marv Penner (Zondervan, 2008)

I Want to Talk with My Teen about Addictions by Megan Hutchinson (Standard Publishing, 2006)

The Youth Worker's Guide to Helping Teenagers in Crisis by Rich Van Pelt and Jim Hancock (Zondervan, 2007)

The Parent's Guide to Helping Teenagers in Crisis by Rich Van Pelt and Jim Hancock (Zondervan, 2007)

Helping Your Struggling Teenager by Dr. Les Parrott III (Zondervan, 2000)

Additional Phone Numbers

Child Pornography Tipline
800-843-5678

National Runaway Switchboard
www.1800runaway.org
800-RUNAWAY

National Suicide Hotline
www.hopeline.com
800-SUICIDE

New Life Ministries Help Line
www.newlife.com
800-NEW-LIFE

Report a Missing Child
www.pollyklaas.org
800-587-4357

CROSSROADS
THE TEENAGE GIRL'S GUIDE TO EMOTIONAL WOUNDS
GOTEE RECORDING ARTIST
Stephanie Smith
& Suzy Weibel